Still Praising Him

Still Praising Him

A Mother's Journey With God

BEV BOWMAN

CURTMAN PUBLISHING
Reed City, MI

Copyright © 2005 Bev Bowman

All rights reserved. No part of this book may be reproduced, stored in a retrieval system, or transmitted in any form by any means electronic, mechanical, photocopying, recording, or otherwise except in brief extracts for the purpose of review, without the permission of the publisher and copyright owner.

Still Praising Him is a work of nonfiction. Some names and identifying details have been changed.

Published by Curtman Publishing
P. O. Box 275
Reed City, MI 49677

Publisher's Cataloging-in-Publication Data
Bowman, Bev.
  Still praising him : a mother's journey with God / Beverly Bowman.
  -- Reed City, MI : Curtman Publishing, 2005.
    p. ; cm.
  ISBN: 0-9767966-0-0
  ISBN-13: 978-0-9767966-0-2

  1. Bowman, Beverly. 2. Faith. 3. Trust in God. 4. Spirituality. 5. Spiritual life--Biblical teaching. 6. Traffic accident victims--Care. 7. Spiritual healing and spiritualism. I. Title.

BV4637 .B69 2005   2005927246
234/.23--dc22   0507

Printed in the United States of America
10 9 8 7 6 5 4 3 2 1

Cover and interior design by To The Point Solutions
www.tothepointsolutions.com

*To my husband, Clois.
We have walked side by side on our rough and
winding journey of life. God has provided strength,
grace, and staying power, which has enabled us to cling
to Him and to each other. The "knot" that tied us
together forty-nine years ago, is still secure. Our
together-forever marriage is, indeed, a God-thing.
Thank you, my precious companion,
for sticking with me through the many challenges life has
presented since we said "I do."
I love you!*

Contents

	PREFACE	9
	ACKNOWLEDGMENTS	13
One	THE LIGHT IS STILL ON	17
Two	SHEILA'S PURSE . . .	25
Three	TIME WENT ON	29
Four	SURVIVE? I DON'T KNOW . . .	37
Five	A NIGHTMARE AND OTHER TOUGH STUFF	45
Six	NOW WHAT?	53
Seven	THE MILES STACK UP	65
Eight	THE "DAILY-NESS" OF LIFE	77
Nine	PRAYER	85
Ten	DEAR GOD, PLEASE GLORIFY YOURSELF	97
Eleven	PEOPLE . . . AND PEACE	103
Twelve	A LONG JOURNEY, INDEED	107

CONTENTS

PRAYER OF PRAISE	125
DEAR READER . . .	133
ABOUT THE AUTHOR	135

POEMS by Bev Bowman

Some Choices Make Life Beautiful . . . Some Choices Break a Heart	39
He Watches From the Shore	49
Each One Holds a Rosebud, Waiting For a Bloom	73
Oh, Pretty Butterfly	84
Jesus, Please Rock Her For Me	110
A Magnificent, Promise-Filled Rainbow	129

Preface

Sheila's purse lay open, with the contents spread over the table. The typical items were there, items one would expect to find in the purse of an eighteen-year-old—a comb, some makeup, pictures, gum. But as I looked over the items, I was excited to find some things that were different from the norm, things that excited me—a book titled, BEING THE WOMAN GOD WANTS ME TO BE. This isn't a book most young ladies carry with them, I thought. Then I noticed the small, ragged-edged squares of paper. "Look, hon! Look at these scraps of paper. I wonder what they are."

Looking closer at the small papers from Sheila's purse, I saw what they were. "Look, hon! These are scripture verses that Sheila wrote out! This thrills me! Listen to this one from Psalm 84:11. It says *'For the Lord God is a sun and shield: the Lord will give grace and glory: no good thing will he withhold from them that walk uprightly.'* And here's Psalm 4:8! It says, *'I will both lay me down in peace, and sleep: for Thou, Lord, only makest me dwell in safety.'"*

Tears coursed down my cheeks as I reread the words. These verses must have been very special and precious to my dear

Sheila. These, and the others she carried, must have provided a stronghold for her. From my perspective, they carried added messages. Questions as well.

We had tagged Sheila as our chatterbox when she was just a child. We knew if she had something on her mind, she would soon be out with it. She had been a child, and a teenager, with a tender heart and conscience. If she felt guilty about something, she would soon confess or apologize—we knew that about our sweet daughter . . . but now, it had been days since she had spoken a word.

A typical girl, Sheila wanted to be pretty. She carefully styled her shoulder-length, soft, brown hair. She plucked her eyebrows and curled her eyelashes. "Mom! Look what I did!" she called out in desperation one day. "I pulled out some eyelashes! Will they grow back?" She was most distressed with what she had done, leaving a "lashless" one-eighth-inch on her eyelid. I assured her they would fill in again.

Within a few weeks, they did grow back. "Sweetie, your eyelashes are all filled in now. They are beautiful! So long and thick. They are beautiful, and so are you!" I told her. But my beautiful daughter made no response. She didn't even open her eyes.

Sheila has been unable to communicate since that terrible night—not even to squeeze my hand, or blink at my command. Not even to ask, "Mom, where am I? What happened to me? Stay with me, Mom. Please, don't leave."

No communication. No answers. Only our tears, sorrow, heartache, and disappointment.

Dear Jesus,

You are the Involved Presence that enables me to face each new day. Thank You, Lord.

Acknowledgments

Thank you, Karen, for encouraging me to "stick to it" and complete this book. It has been in the making for quite a while. Every now and then you have asked, "Have you done any writing this week, Mom? How's your book coming? Getting it about done?"

Up until the last three months I've made excuses, "No, I haven't done any more writing. I've been quite busy. But it's there, waiting for me. I'll get back to it one of these days."

Thank you, Karen, for spurring me on. Your encouragement gave me determination to pursue my writing, and finish the project. You are a precious daughter. I love you.

Thank you, Linda DeMott, for your willingness to read my manuscript. Your comments instilled within me belief that my writing was, indeed, worthwhile. From your insight I understood there truly was strength to be found in reading my book. Your commentary implanted within me confidence that my book would be a resource for direction, encouragement, and endurance. Thank you, Linda, for taking time to read my writings. Thank you for your input. You have encouraged me to see my book through to completion.

Acknowledgments

When a child, you witnessed the onset of our journey, and likely you have been a silent observer from afar, now and again, through the years. More recently, our paths have reconnected. I pray God touched your heart, Linda, as you read the loose pages I handed you. I pray you personally reaped strength and encouragement, as you reviewed my work. Thank you again, and may God bless you!

Thank you, Melissa Langworthy, for your suggestions and critiques, after reviewing what I thought was my nearly complete manuscript. When I approached you about reading it, I detected your anticipation. From your comments, I know you were not disappointed. My book nearly doubled after implementing your suggestions, Melissa! I added information here and there, and it grew! Thank you for your help!

Thank you for the times we have spent together and shared our hearts, my beautiful friend. May God pour His special blessings on you and your family, as you follow Him.

Thank you, Mary Jo, for your expertise in putting my book together into an attractive package. Your knowledge and guidance have been invaluable. Without your help my book would probably still be a dream, not a reality. I'm very thankful Tim referred me to you. May God bless you!

Dear Jesus,
You hold me
In life's hard times.
Thank You, Lord!

One

THE LIGHT IS STILL ON

"I can't sleep, honey. I'm worried about Sheila," I said to Clois, as we lay side by side in bed. "It's after midnight and the kitchen light is still on. Sheila isn't home yet."

Sheila had left home at 5:00 p.m. with Ron and Ken. Ron had come home from college for the weekend, and it was time for him to return. The plan was for the three of them to attend an evening service in Grand Rapids, then deliver Ron to campus. Ken and Sheila would return home after that.

Clois and I went to our evening service. People at church said the weather report was predicting sleet. When I heard that, fear tugged at my heart. The spring-like weather had been beautiful, up in the 70s. Over the winter, Sheila's dad and I had kept a watchful eye on the weather and roads. If it looked bad, we woke Sheila an hour early, so she could ride the ten miles to work with her dad. But now that the weather had improved, we had slacked off on that.

I lay there in bed, filled with concern for Sheila. Fear had a tight grip on my heart. It was dark, except for the dim rays reflected from the kitchen light. Looking at the clock, I noted that it was twenty minutes past midnight.

The shrill ring of the phone startled us. Clois jumped out of bed and hurried to answer it. I immediately sensed the somber tone of the call.

"This is Dr. Johnson, calling from the emergency room in Big Rapids. Do you have a daughter by the name of Sheila?"

"Yes, Sheila is our daughter," Clois said.

Anxiety filled my whole being! Fearful of the message we were about to be given, I was filled with dread, yet impatient to know what was happening with our dear Sheila. The grim expression on Clois's face revealed his heavy concern, and heavy heart, as well.

"Your daughter has been seriously injured in a car accident," the doctor continued. "She's unresponsive, and bleeding from both ears. We need to transfer her to Grand Rapids where they are better equipped to care for her. I need your verbal permission to transfer her. And sir, you need to stay right where you are for now. It's very icy out there. You stay put until the roads are clear."

Clois gave his verbal consent for Sheila's transfer, and the conversation was over. There were no words of encouragement. No details of what had happened. Just a solemn message that gripped our anxious hearts—Sheila was in serious trouble. Clois hung up the phone.

Shocked, and shaking from the dreadful truth we had just been given, we stumbled to the davenport. Our dear Sheila was in trouble. Our fears had become reality. We knelt by the davenport. Through our tears and broken hearts, we placed Sheila in God's care. We couldn't be with her at that time, but we knew He could.

On that nightmare night, April 2, 1978, Sheila was the front seat passenger in a tiny yellow Volkswagon. Just after midnight, when she and her friend were close to home, the car hit a spot of black ice. Spinning out of control, the car was propelled backwards down the road. It collided with a large oncoming car. The impact of the crash wedged Sheila behind the driver. With the thrust of the motion, the left side of her head was slammed against the doorpost. This resulted in a severe closed head injury that left Sheila comatose.

Within a few hours, the roads had cleared somewhat, and we were on our way to the hospital. We had to see Sheila. We had to touch her, and weep beside her.

We finally arrived at Butterworth Hospital in Grand Rapids. Sheila's Uncle Gary, a favorite uncle who was a police officer in East Grand Rapids, met us there. Clois had called him earlier and told him about Sheila.

"I'm just getting off work," Gary said. "I'll go right over to Butterworth. I'll be there when she arrives."

Gary had been by Sheila's side in the emergency room since her arrival. Because of his profession, he was allowed to stay there, while doctors and emergency staff cared for her. Gary met us, quickly filled us in as much as he could, and led us to her room. We peeked inside. Sheila had several machines surrounding her, with a connection leading to each one.

"Are you okay, hon?" I asked Clois, as I looked at his pale face. He quickly lowered himself into a nearby chair and put his head down.

"I was about to faint," he said, in a weak voice. He sat there briefly, until he regained his steadiness.

"Are you going to be all right?" I asked.

"I think so. Just seeing Sheila with all those machines, and the cuts on her face—it almost took me down." He was soon on his feet again, and appeared to be okay.

I turned my attention back to Sheila. "Come on, Sheila. I'll pick you up and take you home, and everything will be all right." It was the initial response of my mother-heart, my attempt to deny reality, I suppose.

But it was evident—the reality of the moment was clearly demonstrated before our eyes. Our sweet Sheila, who just a few hours before had been full of vim and vigor, now lay in Intensive Care, in a small, white, sterile-looking room, with unfamiliar machines ticking, flashing, and beeping information regarding her body systems.

Just a few hours before, Sheila had complimented me on my chocolate chip cookies—"the best ever, Mom!" Later she and I had exercised together to some of her favorite music. Life had suddenly presented us with a mountainous change, a mountainous challenge! We hovered over our sweet Sheila, and wept.

OUR FIRSTBORN, KAREN

Karen was now married and living in Ohio. Shocked and heartbroken to hear about her sister, Karen soon called back to tell us she and her husband, Mark, were coming, and they would arrive early the next morning.

What a comfort it was to have them with us! Karen supported us in our grief, while she hurt intensely herself. Just two weeks earlier she and Mark had been home to visit. Karen and Sheila had talked that Friday night into the wee hours of the morning. Karen didn't know it would be the last time she would ever talk with her sister.

OUR SON, STEVE

Steve turned fifteen a month before Sheila's accident. He found it very hard to face reality. Had we not been so wrapped up in our concern for Sheila, we could have helped him more. But with her ongoing condition, we didn't address Steve's needs.

We feel bad about that, as we look back, but we can't change the past. No, but we can do our best for him now. That is what we strive to do.

Each new day brought fear and dread to our hearts. What will this day hold? we wondered. What will we face today? What will the doctors report to us? Has Sheila made any improvement? Has her condition changed? Has she worsened?

The challenges of Sheila's condition demanded every ounce of strength and courage within us. Clois and I prayed each day, sometimes every hour, to deal with what was before us.

"Sheila will not likely survive," the neurologist told us. "If she does, she will probably be a vegetable."

A vegetable! My Sheila, a vegetable? Don't call her that! How unfeeling! How crass of him! Such thoughts tore through my head. How brash! Doesn't that doctor have any feelings? The doctor's devastating report knocked the props out from under us, destroying even the tiniest shred of hope.

Sorrow ripped at our hearts.

A day later another severe blow. It was abrupt. There was no sensitive lead-in: "Do you wish to donate Sheila's organs?"

Of course, we assumed, when confronted with such a question, that Sheila was not going to make it. The props were knocked out from under us again, and we hit bottom.

"Oh, we aren't saying Sheila is going to die," the nurse said. "There has been no definite change in her condition at this time. This is only a routine question. It's an issue we address so we will be prepared, and know what to do, in case the patient does pass away."

A routine question? By no means! Not for us! We struggled again, to overcome this blow. Maybe it was all in a day's work for the medical staff, but it was not for Mom and Dad, Karen and Steve, and other family members. Not at all!

CRISIS

The waiting room was our "living room" for days on end. A spirit of unity was evident. Everyone there was on common ground, with each person hurting for the others. Heartache tied us all together, and our tears flowed freely.

It was several days into Sheila's injury. She had been laboring to breathe for quite some time. It was heart wrenching to watch her work so hard. After seeing her struggle, I walked out of her room one day, and returned to the waiting room. "I can't go in there and see Sheila again," I moaned. "She's working so hard to breathe. I can't go back! It's too much. It hurts too much. I can't watch her struggle any more," I said.

"You stay here and rest, Mom," Karen said. "We'll keep watch over Sheila." So Karen and her dad took turns going into Sheila's room to check on her. This provided a brief respite for me.

But I couldn't stay away. After a while I cautiously walked into ICU. From a distance I peered into her room. I saw a quiet and still Sheila. What's going on? I wondered. She looks so peaceful. I quickly found Sheila's nurse and inquired.

"Sheila quit breathing a few minutes ago, so we put her on the respirator. She can rest now."

I returned to Sheila's bedside. She looked so calm, so sweet, so beautiful, so precious, as she lay there quiet and still. It was good to see her resting. But what problems would she face with the respirator? Would we, at some time, have to say, "Turn it off"?

The neurologist had said, "The first seven days are crucial. The brain will swell. We don't know how much. We'll watch your daughter closely and give her the very best care available. Her condition is very grim."

For several days, Sheila's life hung in the balance. Finally she began to make slow progress with improvement of her body systems. She relied less and less on the ventilator. At last, she was breathing totally on her own, and able to be weaned from the machine. We rejoiced for the progress she had made. But there were many other concerns.

Sheila still lay motionless, speechless, unresponsive, and helpless.

Two

SHEILA'S PURSE . . .

After several days I left the hospital for a brief time and returned home. Family members had tracked down Sheila's personal items.

With tears streaming down my face I held up the pretty dress she had worn that evening—now split from top to bottom for easier removal from her injured body. There were her black heels and her purse. Sheila's purse! I emptied the contents on the table. Thirstily I searched for any thread of encouragement, of hope, any offering of comfort and consolation.

There they were—little pieces of paper with scripture verses scribbled on them. Tears continued to course down my cheeks as I read the verses again and again. I wondered what they meant for Sheila . . . *"The Lord God is a sun and shield!"* But look where Sheila is! Comatose! A shield? A protector? *"The Lord will give grace and glory?"* Where is the grace? Glory? *". . . no good thing will He withhold from them that walk uprightly."* Sheila was living for Jesus. She was "walking uprightly." I didn't understand.

I read Psalm 4:8: *"I will both lay me down in peace, and sleep: for Thou, Lord, only makest me dwell in safety."* I didn't understand that verse either. Sheila was sleeping—a very deep sleep. She did look peaceful, finally, after a lengthy struggle. Was she "dwelling in safety?" I didn't understand.

I turned again to Psalm 84. I read the complete chapter, searching for a word from the Lord that would minister to the hurt in my heart. I needed something to hold on to. *"Blessed are they that dwell in thy house: they will be still praising Thee. Selah."* (v. 4) I read those words again. God's Spirit seemed to whisper to my spirit, that my praise would please Him. I bowed before God. "Yes, Lord. In spite of Sheila's injury, in spite of my broken heart, I will still be praising Thee."

There were no answers spelled out in bold letters. There was no message of explanation or particular encouragement in what I had just read. But as I analyzed and considered those few words, the response of my heart was "Yes, Lord! I will still be praising Thee!"

Having impressed me to praise Him, God had set my feet on the pathway of healing. He had set my feet in the right direction. I didn't understand that at the time, but as months and years passed, I realized that my God, in all of His knowledge and wisdom, had planted the seed of praise within me—that "watered and nourished" the healing of my broken heart.

"Thank You, Holy Father! I will never cease to praise You! You are always worthy of praise! The circumstances of my life do not change Your Worthy standing! Praise Your Holy Name!"

Holy Father,

Kindle a fire within me for more of You!

Three

Time Went On

Days, weeks, and months passed. Sheila showed no improvement. *"God, I am desperate! I need Your help and Your strength! My heart is broken for my sweet Sheila!"* I prayed and sobbed on my knees beside my bed, until I was physically weak.

I hungrily devoured scripture. I clung to every word of every sermon delivered by a pastor I trusted. I read biographies of those who had experienced God's faithfulness in grievous times. I examined my beliefs. I tore apart what I had been taught through the years. To this point I had accepted those teachings, but I had never put them to the test. Would they hold up in the tragedy that had so suddenly uprooted our family, our home, and our lives?

The clock ticked away the minutes and hours. The calendar pages flipped through the months—and years. Sheila's condition didn't improve. As I looked to God again and again for strength, I found His loving care to be very real. I found His ministry to be tender, gentle, personal, and patient. He presented Himself so quietly, so "in the background." In His wisdom, He mercifully allowed me the grieving time He knew I needed. He knew the heartache of Sheila's injury demanded a large percentage of my energy. But all the time, He was tenderly, gently, and quietly present, slowly effecting a change in me.

AN ELDERLY SAINT OF OUR CHURCH

"I'm praying a portion of Isaiah 61:1 on Sheila's behalf." It was my elderly friend, Blanche, speaking to me. "I'm praying God will free Sheila from her prison."

Yes, without doubt, Sheila was in a type of prison, locked within her body and mind. She couldn't achieve release—by speaking, by hand motions, by eye language, by walking or running. She was definitely confined, definitely imprisoned.

"Thank you so much," I responded. "I appreciate your concern and your prayers more than you will ever know."

"I wonder what the message of that chapter is?" I puzzled, as I awaited opportunity to examine it. "Is there a promise in those verses for Sheila? Do those scriptures hold any gems for me?"

Finally I sat down with my Bible and began to read Isaiah 61. *"The Spirit of the Lord God is upon me; because the Lord hath anointed me . . . ,"* then skipping to verse 3, *"To appoint unto them that mourn in Zion, to give unto them beauty for ashes, the oil of joy for mourning, the garment of praise for the spirit of heaviness; that they might be called TREES OF RIGHTEOUSNESS, the planting of the Lord, that he might be glorified."* [emphasis by capitals mine]

"Lord, that's been my prayer all along, that You might be glorified!" I read the scripture again. Did I read that correctly?

Can it be? God really wants to turn the ashes of my heartache into *beauty*? He really desires to give me the *oil of joy* for my mourning? He wants to give me His *garment of praise* to wear, in exchange for my spirit of heaviness? Can it be? In addition to that, the verse says if I allow God to do that, He will consider me *a tree of righteousness, His planting, that He might be glorified*!

I get it! This is not about me! It is about Him! *"Yes, Lord,"* I prayed. *"Please take the ashes, take my spirit of heaviness, take my mourning. Please place on my shoulders the garment of praise that You have for me! You are Worthy, Lord. You are Sovereign. Even in the hard times of life, You are faithful! I pray, Lord, as I slip my arms into Your praise garment, and wear it, that You will receive glory. I pray I will be strong for You. I pray I will be a tree of righteousness, as Your Word says, firmly planted in You, with roots that go deep."*

Time went on—days, weeks, and months passed. Sheila remained comatose. Nothing changed in her condition. My mother-heart was broken. I had so many hopes and dreams for her. But there she lay, still no recognition, no response, no movement, no words from her lips.

Again I was overcome with discouragement. Sheila's future looked so bleak! Mom and Dad couldn't fix anything! There was nothing we knew about her future. No one had any answers for us. All we could do was wait. And waiting is so difficult!

At that moment of despair God ministered to me. He asked me a question. No, I didn't hear an audible voice, but He spoke to my spirit. (I have learned that God has a way of communicating with His people, making it clear the message is from Him). "But aren't there many things you know for sure about Me?" He asked.

Rather surprised—and excited, I said, *"Yes, Lord. That is true! There are many things I know about You!"*

I quickly found a paper and pencil, and I began to write what

I have later called the FAITH FACTS—those things I KNEW about God. I wrote:

> I know God is faithful.
> I know God has heard our prayers for Sheila.
> I know God loves Sheila more than we do.
> I know God loves us.
> I'm certain God knows all about our heartache.
> I know God wants what is best for Sheila.
> I know God makes no mistakes.

As time went on, God continued to minister to me, always with gentleness and patience. He impressed me through various messages and methods, of His love and His involvement in Sheila's life, and ours. Again and again He revealed to me that my praise was what He desired, that my praise would please Him. I hungrily accepted His encouragement, and continued to wear His garment of praise. But my heartbreak and loss was still intense, and often I found myself beaten down again. With God's help, I would struggle through each period of darkness and, given a little time, be on my feet again.

God grew my faith. I read Genesis, and on into the Old Testament. I saw clearly that God loved the Israelites, His people. It was plain to me that He took care of them. He was patient with them, as they walked away from Him time after time. I was strongly impacted with God's Faithfulness, His Love, His Sufficiency, His Sovereignty, His Worthiness.

Dear Creator-God,

You are my Personal Friend!

Can it be?

Thank You, Lord Jesus!

SOURCE OF ENCOURAGEMENT AND HOPE

Where does one find strength, in the midst of tragic situations? Where does one find words of encouragement? A source of hope? Solidarity and holding power? Can these be found anywhere? A well-stocked bank account doesn't provide the needed "cement" for life at such times. A big, beautiful home doesn't do it. Nor does a sleek and fancy new car, nor beauty, nor popularity. The only lasting, unwavering reservoir warehoused with strength, hope, holding power, encouragement, and "cement" for coping with tragedy, is God and His Word.

"And he shall be like a tree planted by the rivers of water, that bringeth forth his fruit in his season; his leaf also shall not wither; and whatsoever he doeth shall prosper." (Psalms 1:3)

Jeremiah reinforces that verse in chapter 17:7-8: *"Blessed is the man that trusteth in the Lord, and whose hope the Lord is. For he shall be as a tree planted by the waters, and that spreadeth out her roots by the river, and shall not see when heat cometh, but her leaf shall be green; and shall not be careful in the year of drought, neither shall cease from yielding fruit."*

"And the Lord shall guide thee continually, and satisfy thy soul in drought, and make fat thy bones: and thou shalt be like a watered garden, and like a spring of water, whose waters fail not." (Isaiah 58:11)

These words don't speak of one victimized by life's tragedies. They speak of victory in and through tragedy. I saw God's sufficiency in the words I read! I remembered the *"tree of righteousness, the planting of the Lord,"* in Isaiah 61.

In these scriptures I read about the *tree planted by the rivers of water*—abundance! Sufficiency! God is sufficient! His Word tells me so! I believe it!

HOW LONG, LORD?

After weeks, months, years, my sweet Sheila is still confined to bed. She never utters a word. Most of the time she looks comfortable and at peace. This is a different Sheila—not our vivacious second-born, full of chatter, always concerned about the welfare of others.

No, this Sheila is totally dependent on others for her every need. In many respects, she is like my baby. To me, she is beautiful. Since her injury, her eyes don't work together. Her facial features are sometimes contorted into ugly expressions. Sometimes she drools. But to me, she is precious and beautiful. "I love you, sweetie! Mom loves you!" I tell her often, but she makes no response.

She never squeezes my hand, as if to say, "Thanks, Mom." She just lies there, positioned as her caregiver placed her. In two hours she will be repositioned . . . for two more hours.

DISAPPOINTMENT EXPRESSED

"Lord, I had hopes and dreams for Sheila. I envisioned that someday she would marry a fine young man, and when the time was right, their love would produce precious grandchildren for Grandpa and me."

I didn't want it to be this way. Were my plans and dreams better? Is Sheila's situation all in God's plan? Did God cause this? As I searched scripture, I came to understand that, for some reason, God had allowed this to happen. He didn't cause it. He wasn't surprised by the ice on the highway that night. He wasn't suddenly frustrated. He didn't wring His hands and wonder what to do to protect her from danger. No, I reasoned, because our world is a sinful place, these things happen. There was no question in my mind whether God could have prevented the accident. I knew He could have, but for some reason He didn't. He allowed it.

GOOD, FROM TRAGEDY?

With the passing of years, I understood that God, in His infinite wisdom, would bring about good through this tragedy, as Romans 8:28 says. I did not read into this that God would make Sheila whole again, from an earthly standpoint. Accepting this verse as truth didn't take care of all the unknowns or all the questions. The messages I received were messages of encouragement: "Trust God." "God is faithful." "God loves Sheila." "God is involved in all the details of your lives. Trust Him."

I came to the place of believing that God is a loving, faithful, just, and sovereign God. Somehow, He is taking care of everything. I accepted and believed those truths He had planted in my heart, as I searched for Him, and His truth. I believed them through my own tried-and-true experience. They weren't hand-me-downs any longer. I had tested them in the crucible of tragedy. They had passed the tests! They were mine!

Four

SURVIVE? I DON'T KNOW . . .

Hearing a car, I look out the front window. I am shocked to see a police car pull into the driveway! I watch, dumbfounded, as two more patrol cars drive in!

With anxious and pounding heart, I observe an officer as he gets out of his car, and walks toward the front door. I open the door in response to his knock.

"Hello, Mrs. Bowman. I'm Officer Crandall. Is your son Steve home? I would like to speak with him."

"Yes, Steve is here. I'll call him." I go to Steve's room and tell him the law officer wants to talk to him. When Steve approaches the door, the officer asks him to come outside. I follow. We form a circle in front of the garage. They talk. I listen. "Mrs. Bowman," an officer soon speaks to me. "Would you please go back inside? We need to talk with your son alone."

I return to the house and watch. In a short time the officer comes back to the door. "We've arrested your son, Mrs. Bowman. We're taking him with us. Would you like to call your husband? Can you contact him?"

With shaking hands I pick up the phone and dial our church number, where Clois is working. It seems to take forever for him to answer, but finally I hear his voice on the other end of the line.

"Hello. This is Clois speaking."

"You need to come home right away," I blurt out between my sobs. "Steve has just been arrested and they are taking him away."

"What? Arrested? I'll be right home," Clois said. I hear the click of the phone as he hangs up.

By this time Steve is in handcuffs, sitting in the back of the sheriff's car. An officer asks Steve if he wants to wait until his dad arrives. He says no.

Devastated, I watch as the three cars pull out of our driveway and take my son away, to jail. It is a nightmare . . . acted out . . . But no, this one is for real too—just as real as Sheila's injury seven years ago. In all of my mom-worries, I had not come up with this one. Powerful emotions overtake me—sorrow, hurt, disappointment, embarrassment, shame, sadness.

Unstoppable tears flow from my eyes.

Some Choices Make Life Beautiful . . .
Some Choices Break a Heart

I.
Springtime and its beauty
Surround me everywhere,
As leaves unfold in mystery
And blossoms dress each branch that was bare.

Boring lawns become green with new life,
Bulbs buried deep send shoots toward the light,
Sleeping plants awaken,
Leaving behind the darkness and night.

Wooded havens come alive as they bud and bloom,
Wild flowers flaunt their lovely heads,
Floral bushes show undergarments of green,
And mushrooms spring up from their earthen beds.

God's world around me is royally dressed
In regal springtime freshness and beauty,
Shouting to me, "Note my designer wardrobe—
God's design! It's a joy to wear! Not a duty!"

Gardens soon will boast promise of veggies—
Of green, bright red, and pearly white—
With flowers of every color and description—
Variety is a gardener's wish and delight!

II.
Long ago there was a garden—remember?
It was exquisite! Abundant! Deep green, and lush!
Except for the animals and the bird songs,
The garden was covered with a holy hush.

Adam walked in that magnificent garden.
God saw Adam's heart there—God walked there, too!
He knew his man, Adam, was very lonely—
"I'll make him a companion—that's what I will do!"

Adam's eyelids became heavy, so Adam took a nap.
God opened his side, and removed a bone,
From it made Eve—a lovely, baffling woman!
No longer would Adam be lonely, no longer he'd be alone!

Just imagine, will you, Adam's surprise
When he saw this lovely girl!
How God loved him to recognize his need
And create this one who would set his head awhirl!

Adam and Eve lived in that alluring garden
Where there was beauty beyond compare!
Only one restriction was theirs to consider—
But that limitation was, for Eve, a snare.

Eve made a tragic, devastating choice—
She rejected God, believing rather, the snake.
Could she possibly have known
What disastrous changes her decision would make?

Please know—the everyday choices of life are important!
They may build lives, or tear them apart!
Consider your choices—pray, and weigh them—
Some choices make life beautiful; some choices break a heart!

I couldn't stand being alone in our empty house. It was too painful! I didn't want to face people. Newspaper and media coverage had spilled the details to the whole community. We were on display again, for everyone to see. I knew it would be hard to face my fellow employees, but I had no choice. I couldn't stand it at home, so I went back to work.

Clois worked long days. After completing his workday, he put in four or five hours on a building project at church. This was therapy for him, but his long hours left me alone every evening. It was tough. I didn't know if I was going to hold myself together or not.

Each day after work, and after spending time with Sheila, I went home to an empty house. My tears flowed freely. I couldn't stop them. My mother-heart was broken. There seemed to be no help anywhere in this foreign world of arrest, jail, incarceration, judges, criminal lawyers, guilty/not guilty pleas, plea bargaining, bold newspaper articles, and TV coverage. It was an ugly road we had never traveled before—a muddy, rut-filled, deep-ditch road—a road we did not want to travel. But whether we wanted to or not, that's where we were—stuck on a road that led nowhere but to more heartache and despair.

Intense emotions accompanied us everywhere, as we walked that lonely road. Wherever we went, we felt the eyes of everyone upon us. We were the topic of all surrounding conversations—we just knew it. We were living under a heavy burden, and it was a struggle.

Then, one day in my sorrow and depression, God showed up again! He communicated with me—His Spirit with my spirit. I heard no audible voice. I heard nothing with my ears, but I definitely understood that He was communicating with me. Once again, He asked me a question. "Don't you think it's time to praise me? You've been so focused on your heartache, it has clouded your vision for everything else. Don't you think it's time to look to Me, and praise Me?"

"*Yes, Lord. You are right,*" I responded. "*It is time to praise You!*" In spite of, and in the midst of the tragedy of my son's crime, I began to praise the Lord. When the pastor asked for testimonies the following Sunday night, I stood on my feet and gave praise to my Lord.

Looking back, I know God was with me all the time. But I was swallowed up in the intensity of the whole, ugly situation—so much so, that my vision was blurred. I couldn't see Him.

Dear Lord,

The welcome mat is out for You.

I invite You to every moment of my life!

Five

A Nightmare and Other Tough Stuff

Steve's court date was fast approaching. We faced it with dread. "I'm afraid of what tomorrow will bring. I'm so fearful of what Steve's sentence will be."

Concern was clearly evident on Clois's face, as he listened and nodded his head in agreement with me. He was feeling the same apprehension.

Never, at any time, had we believed Steve should go free. He had to pay for what he had done. We knew that. He knew it, too. But our hope was that his sentence would be comparable to the sentences of others guilty of similar crimes.

The clock ticked away the hours of our worrisome day. "Let's go to bed," Clois said. "There's nothing we can do but trust the Lord with this. We can't change a thing."

We soon climbed into bed for the night, but sleep didn't come for me. Troubling thoughts regarding Steve's sentencing kept me awake and tense, tossing and turning. Finally I dozed off . . . only to have a nightmare—not a real-life event this time, but most definitely a dreadful nightmare—

I find myself standing at the main intersection in the nearby town where Steve is incarcerated. I look out in the street. I can't believe what I'm seeing! "Oh, no! There's a baby crawling out in the street! This is a main intersection! Help! Help, somebody! There's a baby out there under the light! Someone will run over him! He'll be killed! Help! Help!"

I look closer. "No! No! It can't be!" I shout, shaking my head in horror and disbelief. "It looks like my little Andy! My little grandson! No! It can't be! It can't be!"

In my agonizing weakness I stumble and fall against the corner light post. The lights of an approaching car reflect from the window of a corner store, and alert me to imminent danger. Struggling to stand to my feet, suddenly I am frozen with distress, as I watch my fears play out. "No, no, no!" I scream. "Don't run over the baby!" I yell hysterically. "Don't run over him!"

Clumsily I run into the intersection, putting forth every bit of strength I can muster. The scene takes my breath. A mournful groan comes from deep within me. "They did! They ran over him! They ran over my little Andy!" I whisper. "They ran over him." Sobbing uncontrollably, I fall to the street and bury my head in my arms. Mournful sounds come from deep within me, expressive of my inconsolable sorrow.

At last I raise my head and glance around. "What is that little pile over there? There's one over that way too. What are they?" Curious, I crawl to inspect them. "No! No!" I moan. "Oh, please, no!" Overcome with grief, I slump into a shivering, sobbing, despairing heap—having discovered the little piles to be parts of my little Andy's body.

That dreadful nightmare depicted my desperate and hopeless

frame of mind. Everything looked so desolate and black! My mother-heart would not be consoled.

The next day, nine months after Steve's arrest, he was sentenced to many years in prison. He was given a harsh sentence. That same day he was transferred to Jackson State Prison, one hundred and fifty miles from home. We were devastated.

"Let's go to Karen's for the weekend," Clois said. "I think it would do us good to get away and not have to face everyone for a while." We quickly made arrangements and left home, eager to avoid the embarrassment, the questions, the stares, and the curiosity of the community. We headed for Ohio to spend a few days with Karen, Mark, and little Andy. Only a few of Karen's friends there would know what was going on in our lives, not the whole community.

Jackson Prison was located on the direct route we traveled. We knew nothing about prisons, their visiting guidelines, or anything else connected with them. We had been told new prisoners spend a couple of weeks in quarantine, and that they cannot have visitors during that time. But we decided to give it a try. If we could see Steve, great. If not, at least we would be comforted to some degree, knowing we had made the effort.

"We're here to see Steve Bowman," Clois told the officer at the desk. "He just arrived here yesterday. We don't know if he is allowed to have a visit yet or not, but if so, we want to see him." We were happily surprised when the officer responded positively. He provided us with minimal information and then told us to sit in the waiting area across the room. He said when Steve was brought into the visiting room we would be called and they would take us in.

After we waited a half-hour our name was called. We rose, on edge with anxiety, and followed the guard. What are we getting into? We each saw the apprehension in the other's eyes, as the huge doors clanged shut behind us.

We were directed to walk through the metal detector, and then to submit to being frisked. When that was done, we were escorted to the area where we would see Steve. The place was a dungeon! How devastating it was to walk into that crowded visiting room, to see Steve there, and know he would be there for a very long time . . . it broke my mother-heart again.

He Watches From the Shore

Have you ever felt your boat of life
Was far out in a storm-ravaged sea,
Bobbing around, running off course,
When peace was your heartfelt plea?

It seemed strong winds had forced your little boat
To follow an unknown course,
Until you felt you were exhausted and spent,
And had depleted every hope and resource.

The storm came up when the illness struck,
Or perhaps you were troubled by a child's decision—
When you knew your aging parents needed you more—
A peaceful life was not within your vision.

The roof on the house had served twenty-five years,
Appliances demanded replacement or repair,
The car was nearing the peak mileage range,
The siding on the house was looking old and bare.

When your lifeboat was tossed about this way and that—
Did you feel helpless and out of control?
As you struggled in vain to get back on course,
Did you feel stressed, knowing stress takes its toll?

Let me encourage you from Mark chapter 6,
Let me offer you hope, when life's strong winds blow—
Let me help you understand—peace in your lifeboat
Doesn't always depend on how hard you row.

Once twelve men were in a boat
Far out in the middle of the lake.
The wind was powerful and in command—
In the storm they feared their lives were at stake.

Back on shore, the Master was aware—
He was watching the storm. He understood their fright.
He saw their struggle as they strained against the oars,
Trying desperately, stretching their muscle and might.

The Master knew the storm alarmed them,
He knew their fears, their strength was wearing thin.
His heart of love moved Him—He walked on the water!
Then, reaching their boat, HE CLIMBED IN!

Amazement was theirs—The Master walked on water!
The wind died down. Peace flooded their hearts again!
Calmly they manned the oars!
Their Master was near, and He was in command!

When you are challenged by life's storms, straining at the oars
To keep your little boat on course,
You know you are no match for the wind—
You know its powerful force,

Remember the Master is watching from the shore!
He knows your strength and hope are wearing thin.
Remember the Master can walk on water!
He will walk to your lifeboat, and then He'll climb in!

You will be so blessed when you find the Master near!
Sweet peace will flood your heart again.
He's been there all the time, but now you recognize His
    Presence—
And you know He's in command!

(Based on Mark 6:45-52)

Dear Lord,

May I never cease to be amazed

At Your Presence,

Your involvement,

In my life.

Six

NOW WHAT?

I wonder why Clois is sitting on the well curb out there. It's unusual for him to stop and sit down when he's in the middle of mowing the lawn. I know he wants to get it done this morning. Maybe he's just checking out something.

I go on about my work, hoping to accomplish a lot before noon. Everything seems normal, until I walk by the window and see him there again, sitting on the well curb. I run to the door and call out to him, "Are you okay, hon? Is something wrong?"

"I just had to stop and rest," Clois said. "My chest is really heavy. It's happened twice since I started mowing the lawn."

"You'd better come in and sit down for a while, hon." Anxiety welled up within me. "Can you make it? Do you need help?"

"No, I'm feeling better now. I'm okay." We go inside and he sits down in the recliner.

"I think you'd better see the doctor. We need to find out what's going on, especially with all the heart problems in your family. What do you think?" With a worrisome look on his face, he agrees.

The next several days were busy with doctors, a stress test, referral to a Grand Rapids cardiologist, and further testing there. During those days, his chest heaviness returned intermittently . . . then came the alarming diagnosis. "Four of your arteries are blocked, two of them severely. One is almost totally obstructed, so much so that your blood flow has made its own collateral pathway. That's what has prevented you from having a heart attack. You are a walking time bomb, Mr. Bowman."

Clois lay on the bed, recuperating from the catheterization procedure. I held his hand, as I stood beside his bed. Oh! Such a disturbing report! The cardiologist continued, "There is no question about it, Mr. Bowman. You definitely are in need of urgent bypass surgery." Stunned, we questioned the cardiologist regarding possible options. He told us there really were no options at this point. We presented our concerns to him, and after much discussion and consideration, Clois made the decision to proceed with surgery. From his experience over the last several days, he knew he, indeed, had a problem.

"We will schedule your surgery for 8:00 a.m. tomorrow. We have several surgeons in our office," the cardiologist said, as he handed Clois a pamphlet. "Do you have a preference?" We perused the information. The name of one surgeon did stand out, and Clois advised the doctor of our selection.

"You will be transferred to a room on the surgical floor. I'll contact Dr. Chaney. He'll be in to see you in the late afternoon. In the meantime, you stay in bed. Don't even put your feet on the floor!" Dr. Frank walked over to Clois's bedside and reached out to shake his hand. "It's a good thing you saw your doctor when you began to experience the chest heaviness. You were certainly on the road to a heart attack. I hope all goes well for you." He shook Clois's hand, and mine, and left the room.

There we were, facing yet another crisis—a sudden turn of events. This was major surgery we were looking at, and it was scheduled for tomorrow morning! I breathed a prayer, *"Heavenly Father, we need You!"*

Nursing staff soon came to transfer Clois to his room. When he was settled in, they began the necessary preparations for surgery. Occasionally, during the next few hours, we were left alone, to discuss our concerns and what needed to be done.

Karen had to be informed of these latest developments. I picked up the phone on the bedside stand and dialed her number. She was at work, I knew, but she answered right away. "Hi, Karen," I responded to her cheery voice. "I'm calling to tell you the latest developments with Dad. He's facing bypass surgery in the morning, Karen."

"He's what? Did you say he is facing surgery in the morning? What kind of surgery?" I heard the bewilderment in her voice.

"Yes, Karen. Dad is facing heart bypass surgery—four bypasses. It's scheduled for eight tomorrow morning. We are at Blodgett Hospital in Grand Rapids. Dad has a room on the surgical floor. He is being prepared for surgery now. We haven't talked to the surgeon yet, but he will be in to speak with us soon."

"We're coming up, Mom," Karen said, with heavy concern in her voice. "We're going to be there with you. I'll call Mark, and we'll make arrangements. How can I let you know the details when we get it all figured out?" I gave Karen the number of Dad's room. When I told him they were coming, he was so thankful. I made more calls to family, and to our pastor. Several I called said they would be there to wait through the surgery with me.

A short time later the surgeon slipped into the doorway. "Mr. Bowman?" he asked. Receiving an affirmative response, he proceeded to explain what lay ahead. In his hand he held a picture of a heart. The arteries were displayed, and by each of the four blocked arteries the percentage of obstruction was written. He explained the necessity of surgery, and the procedure. Patiently he answered our questions and calmed our anxieties. We were strongly impressed that he knew the procedure well. "Any more concerns?" he asked, as he rose from his chair. By that time we had asked all the questions we could think of. "I'll see you in the morning, Mr. Bowman." Turning to me, he said, "We'll take good care of him, Mrs. Bowman."

Karen called later in the afternoon with everything arranged. They would arrive late, and spend the night at Uncle Gary and Aunt Virg's home. Little Andy would stay with them, while Karen and Mark came to the hospital.

It was getting late . . . 8:00 a.m. would be here all too soon. I bid good-bye to Clois, assured him I would be there early in the morning, and left. Sleep didn't come easily for me—or for him.

In spite of my anxieties, the night passed quickly and I soon found myself back at Clois's bedside. Karen and Mark, other family members, and friends began to filter in. Several pastors had arrived. As the scheduled time for surgery approached, the pastors surrounded Clois's bed to pray with him—just in time, for as soon as they were finished, surgical staff arrived to take Clois to the next level for further prep, and to await transfer to the surgical suite. He was medicated by now, and drifting in and out. On schedule, he was wheeled into surgery. We returned to the surgical waiting room. It would be a long wait.

Intermittently we were informed of how Clois was doing, and the progress of the procedure. It was such a long wait! I was thankful for the concern everyone expressed by their presence. It was very supportive for me to have friends and family near.

Well, it was finally over! In spite of his appearance—shocking, with all of the tubes and connections—the surgeon reported that the surgery went very well.

Clois's recuperation was right on schedule, as the days passed, with no complications. He improved, meeting the hospital's established timing and goals. Both he and I sat in on "after bypass surgery" instructions. Prescribed medications were discussed. The importance of a walking program was presented to us, and we were given a plan to follow. "It is imperative that you walk regularly," the surgeon told Clois. "It is as important as any of your medications. You must walk!"

Clois was dismissed from the hospital on schedule. How thankful we were to the medical staff for their knowledge, expertise, and good work. But we knew the Great Physician! We knew He had a hand in all that had transpired over the last few weeks.

"Thank You, Holy Father! You are the Great Physician! Healing comes from You, and You alone. We can't thank You enough, Lord! You are faithful! Praise Your Name!"

BLESSING, IN THE MIDST OF IT ALL

We didn't know it at the time, but wrapped up in this whole disquieting package, was a blessing for us. Clois had been given a prescription to walk regularly. So, he walked. And I walked. Over the next several weeks we built up our walking time to one hour a day. During that time, Clois and I talked. That would never have happened, had we not been out walking. We had time to discuss everything, time to talk over our concerns for Sheila and Steve, time to discuss our disagreements. Walking together has been good for Clois's heart health, and for mine. But, in addition, it has been a source of therapy for our marriage. It provides opportunity for "marriage enrichment."

Statistics for marriage failure hang around 80 percent when a couple is faced with tragedy. After Sheila's injury our sorrow drew us closer, as together we depended on the Lord for strength. Steve's arrest was a totally different thing to handle. We struggled through the first year. Then Clois's surgery zoomed into the picture. After that came the prescription for walking. It was marriage therapy, a marriage enrichment class, a time to communicate, as Clois (and I) followed doctor's orders—WALK!

Clois's surgery was June 1986. We're still walking together in 2005. We still need marriage therapy. We still need time to communicate—always will. Our marriage is good. And God is good!

DEALING WITH ANGER

While Clois was in the intensive care unit recovering from heart surgery, friends and family members stopped by to see us, and to wish him well. We were pleasantly surprised one day when a psychologist friend appeared in the doorway. "Hey, Bob! It's good to see you!" Clois said, as he extended his hand to greet Bob.

"Wow, it's good to see you, Clois! You're looking super! You too, Bev!" Bob looked around the room. "This is a nice apartment you have here. You aren't planning on staying here, are you?" Bob grinned, as he sat down in the bedside chair.

"Oh, no! I'm not staying here." Clois sat up and swung his feet around to sit on the side of the bed. "It's a marvelous place to be when you need it. The staff has done a great job of taking care of me, but I don't want to hang around here. You know, there's no place like home, Bob."

The three of us chatted for a while; then Bob rose from his chair. "I'd better be on my way. I don't want to wear you out, Clois. I'm really pleased to see you looking so good! Your assignment now is to take it easy, so your body can heal from the surgery. Bev will see to that, I'm sure." Bob grinned, as he shook hands with each of us. Then he turned and walked toward the door. Lingering in the doorway, he spoke to me. "May I talk to you a minute, Bev?" he asked.

"Sure," I answered, and followed him into the hallway.

With a soft voice, Bob spoke slowly and cautiously. "It seems to me that as you speak about Steve's situation and how the courts handled his case, I recognize anger in you, Bev."

I quickly responded in denial. "No, Bob. I'm not angry. I don't like the way the courts dealt with some issues, but I'm not angry. I could meet any one of the court officials on the street, and look him in the eye, and shake hands with him. I'm not angry."

Bob nodded. "All right, Bev. I thought I detected anger in you, but I guess I misjudged you. Anger is often a problem when dealing with hard situations. But it sounds like you are doing well."

"Thank you for your willingness to help, Bob. I really do appreciate your concern," I said.

"Well, I'll be on my way now. My wife has a honey-do list waiting for me, as usual." Bob smiled and turned to leave.

"Thanks for coming, Bob. Your visit was a blessing to us." I waved and turned into the doorway of Clois's room.

In the following few days Clois did very well and was soon discharged to go home. How thankful we were for his new lease on life.

As the weeks passed, I thought about what Bob had said. Anger? Bitterness? No, not me. I'm not filled with anger. I confess I do not like some of the things the court officials did, but they have a difficult job. They have to make some tough decisions. I admit I do not like the way Bruce and Marie dealt with Steve's situation, but I'm not harboring anger against them either.

Throughout the following months I continued to deny that I had feelings of anger. But finally I began to question myself. Why do I want to do this? Why do I want to do that? Why do certain thoughts keep popping into my mind? Why can't I dismiss those thoughts once and for all? Why do I keep replaying certain events in my mind? Why do I keep nursing my hurt?

After much soul searching and inward reflection, I concluded that Bob was correct in his assessment. There was anger within me. I was angry with four particular individuals, two in the court system and two outside. From past experience, I knew that anger and bitterness were heavy baggage to carry. I knew that carrying a load of anger hurts the one who carries it more than it hurts those it is directed toward. And I knew I could not carry a load of anger and bitterness, along with the burdens I was already carrying—due to no choice of my own—and survive. So I prayed.

"Lord, You have helped me understand that I am filled with anger toward some individuals who, I feel, did not deal with Steve's case in the way they should have. But I can't carry that burden of anger, Lord. The load I am forced to carry is very heavy, as it is. I can't carry another one! Please help me, Lord. I'll do my part. Whenever thoughts come into my mind about these individuals and events, I will immediately dismiss them. Beginning now, I will not dwell on such thoughts! Lord, I promise to be faithful with this. Please, will You heal me of my anger? Will You help me forgive these people? Will You heal me so completely that the thoughts of anger will no longer come to my mind? Thank You, Lord. I know I can trust You. I know You will do Your part. If anyone fails, it will be me. Praise Your Holy Name. Amen."

I was determined to be true to my promise to God, and I was. Whenever thoughts of those individuals and disturbing situations came to my mind, I dismissed them at once, and focused my thoughts on something else. I didn't keep a record of the number of days or weeks it required, but it wasn't very long before my burden was gone! What a relief! What a release!

"Holy Father, thank You! You helped me follow through on my promise! And You did Your part—of course You did! You took my burden, Lord! Thank You! Thank You for Your faithfulness! Thank

You for Your mercy and grace! What freedom I have! Thank You, Holy Father!"

How often anger wants to show its ugly head. The circumstances don't have to be anything as huge as mine. Situations of much lesser degree can create such a problem, if anger is allowed to get a foothold.

In two separate instances several years ago, I felt I was treated unfairly and given no consideration. These situations were simple, everyday-type occurrences—nothing like Steve's problem, which really sent me tumbling head over heels. I remember playing the events of the circumstances over and over in my mind—what the other person said, what she did, her stance during the encounter . . . As I dealt with the troubling issues, I laid out some facts and guidelines for dealing with anger:

- Replaying the situation is like putting fertilizer on a plant. It causes the situation to grow within a person's mind. The whole thing is nurtured and blown out of proportion.
- Anger will consume me. It will never go away, as long as I cuddle and nurse it.
- My strong and troublesome feelings of anger are my problem. The one(s) I feel is at fault is probably totally unaware I am having difficulty dealing with the event and is probably unaware of doing or saying anything wrong. She has very likely forgotten the whole thing.
- I am the loser if I continue to harbor anger.
- I must release my anger—the whole package—to God. I must not allow such thoughts any room in my mind.
- I must ask God for help to get rid of my burden of anger.

After I finally figured out my true feelings, I admitted I had a problem. Once again, God was faithful. He gave me wisdom to know what to do in my place of need. I followed through and God wiped the slate clean! My anger was gone! My heart was free again!

The important thing for me to do in dealing with anger, is to keep my heart in tune with God, through consistent connection with Him—prayer, scripture reading, singing of hymns and praises, and inspirational reading—through every available opportunity. If I keep close to Him, He will help me prevent anger from inching its way in. Keeping my heart in tune with God requires a relationship with Him! A relationship with Him requires consistent connection!

Dear Lord Jesus,
May I recognize Your hand
In the many small miracles
Of each new day.

Seven

THE MILES STACK UP

We visited Steve weekly for the two years he was in Jackson State Prison. It was three hundred miles roundtrip, and it was hard. However, we were determined to preserve what was left of our son.

Karen's firstborn, Andrew Lee, was born on August 28, 1984, not quite a year before Steve's arrest. Sometimes we would all visit Steve—Karen, Mark, Andy, and us.

Jackson Prison's visiting arrangements were not toddler-friendly. Seats were assigned in the visiting room. There was no roaming around. Even young children had to stay put. How do you keep a little one quiet for two hours? Clois and I saw Steve weekly, much more often than Karen and Mark could. So, when they met us there, I made it my responsibility to entertain little Andy. I would hold him on my lap and whisper in his ear, making up stories as I talked. I remember one . . .

JOHNNY VISITS THE FARM

Johnny was sleeping in bed one morning. His Daddy went into his room. "Johnny! Wake up! We're going to visit Farmer Brown! We'll watch him milk the cows! He's going to show us all of his animals. You'll see cows and horses and pigs and chickens and dogs and kitty cats! Come on, Johnny! Wake up! We don't want to be late!"

"I'm tired, Daddy. I don't wanna get up!"

Johnny's daddy leaned over the bed and scooped Johnny up in his big arms. "Ah, come on, Johnny! Let's go in the bathroom. I'll wash your face, and then I'll help you get dressed. You want to see Farmer Brown's farm, I know! Okay?"

"Okay, Daddy, but I'm really tired." Johnny laid his head on his daddy's big shoulder. He didn't even open his eyes. He was so sleepy!

Daddy carried Johnny into the bathroom, and set him on the potty. When Johnny was done, Daddy set him up by the sink, and washed his face and hands, and combed his hair. Then Daddy carried Johnny back to his bedroom and found some clothes. Johnny yawned. He stretched, and leaned on Daddy, while Daddy dressed him—pants and shirt, then socks and shoes. Daddy found Johnny's favorite baseball cap and put it on his head. "There, captain! We're ready! Let's find Mama and tell her good-bye. Mama's not going with us. It's just you and me today, Johnny! We won't eat breakfast here. Mrs. Farmer Brown is going to fix breakfast for us, buddy. Besides, you're too sleepy to eat now, right, Johnny?" Johnny nodded his head.

Daddy carried Johnny to Mama, and they told her good-bye. Mama gave both of them a big kiss. Daddy took Johnny out to the car, and put him in the car seat. "Hey, there, boy! Let's go, okay?"

"Okay, Daddy. Let's go see Farmer Brown and his animals." Daddy thought Johnny was finally beginning to wake up.

It didn't take long to get to Farmer Brown's barn. Daddy stopped the car and unbuckled Johnny from his car seat. "Here we are, Johnny Boy! Let's go see the cows! Are you ready?"

"Yeah, Daddy! I'm ready! Let's go see 'em cows! I like cows, Daddy!" Johnny was awake now! He was getting excited!

Daddy walked through the big barn door. He looked down the aisle and saw Farmer Brown. "Hey, good morning, Farmer Brown! We're here to see your farm! Sure are glad you invited us, aren't we, Johnny?"

Johnny nodded his head. He was excited! "Look, Daddy! The cows are big! Lotsa cows, right, Daddy?"

"That's right, son! There are lots of cows, and they are big! There are black and white cows, and brown cows."

Daddy stepped up closer to where Farmer Brown was milking a black and white cow. There was a kitty close to Farmer Brown. Farmer Brown squirted milk from the cow, right into the kitty's mouth. Oh! The kitty liked that! He lapped up the milk. "Look, Daddy! Kitty likes the milk. Right, Daddy?"

"Yup! He sure does like that milk. Milk is good for him, Johnny. You like milk, too, don't you? Milk is good for you, too." Farmer Brown stopped squirting the kitty. Then the kitty licked his paws and washed his face.

Farmer Brown worked until he had milked all the cows. Johnny and his daddy watched as Farmer Brown poured the milk into big cans. "What do you think about that, Johnny?" Daddy asked. "That's a lot of milk, isn't it?"

"Yeah, Daddy. That's a lot of milk. We couldn't drink that much, could we, Daddy?"

"No, son," Daddy laughed, "we couldn't drink that much milk."

Farmer Brown took Johnny and his daddy to see the horses. "Look at the horses, Johnny," Farmer Brown said. "Do you like horses?" Johnny nodded his head.

"I like horses, Farmer Brown. I like those ones, and I like those black ones. But they are too big, Farmer Brown! Too big for me!"

Farmer Brown chuckled. "Oh, you think they are too big, huh? Would you like to sit on a horse? Would you like to sit on this black horse, Johnny?" Johnny's eyes widened. He looked up at his daddy.

"It's okay, Johnny. Farmer Brown will help you, if you want to sit on the horse." Johnny looked at Daddy, then he looked at Farmer Brown. He didn't know if he wanted to sit on that tall horse or not! It looked scary!

"Do you want to sit on the horse, Johnny? Come on. I'll help you," Farmer Brown said again.

Johnny wasn't sure. The black horse was so big! But finally he decided he wanted to do it. "Okay. Daddy, will you help me?"

"Sure, I will, Johnny. I'll carry you right over by the horse, and Farmer Brown will help you." The three of them walked to the big black horse. Farmer Brown took Johnny in his arms and carried him up close to the horse.

"He's a nice horse, Johnny. His name is Star. Do you want to pet him? Reach your hand out, like this, and pet him. He'll like that. Then I'll put you on his back, and I'll hold onto you." Farmer Brown reached out and petted the horse. Slowly Johnny reached out his hand too. Cautiously he laid his hand on the horse. Farmer Brown let Johnny pet the horse for a minute, then he carefully lifted Johnny up, and set him on Star's back. "How's that, little fella? How do you like that?"

Johnny's eyes were big! He was way up high on Star! Star was a big horse! "Look at me, Daddy! I'm way up here! This is a big horse! This is Star, Daddy! I like Star!"

After Johnny had sat on the horse for a few minutes, Farmer Brown said, "I think we'd better go see the pigs and chickens now. Mrs. Farmer Brown is getting breakfast for us. She's gonna stick her head out that back door any minute and call us to come in and eat! She makes a good breakfast, Johnny! When she says it's ready, we want to go eat it, don't we?"

Johnny nodded his head. "Yup. When Mrs. Farmer Brown is ready, I want to eat. Are you hungry, Farmer Brown? Are you hungry, Daddy? I'm hungry. I heard my tummy growl!" Johnny laughed. He put his hand on his tummy, as Farmer Brown carried him over to where he could watch the pigs.

"Oink, oink, oink, yourself, piggies," Farmer Brown said. "You aren't hungry. You just ate your breakfast!" He looked at Johnny. "What do you think of these pigs, Johnny? They're fat, aren't they? Do you like pigs, Johnny?"

Johnny looked the pigs over. He pointed to this one and that one. He chuckled, as one pig rooted in the dirt. "He's all dirty, Daddy! He's playing in the mud! I think piggies like to play in the mud, Daddy."

"You're right, son. Pigs like that. The mud cools them off when they're hot. And I think pigs just like to be dirty, don't you, Johnny?"

"Yup, Daddy. I think pigs just like to be dirty!" Johnny repeated.

"Look, Johnny," Farmer Brown said. "See the chickens over here in the chicken coop? What do you think of these girls? Do you suppose we could find an egg anywhere? Did you know chickens give us eggs, Johnny?" Farmer Brown walked over to a shelf-kind-of-place, where a hen perched. "Do you have an egg for me today, Henrietta Hen? How about an egg for Farmer Brown?" He reached under the chicken. He pulled out two eggs! "Look, Johnny! Look at these eggs! Henrietta Hen just gave me two eggs! What do you think about that?"

Johnny's eyes were big! "Look, Daddy! Farmer Brown gots two eggs from Henwi- from that chicken!"

"Sure thing!" Daddy said. "Farmer Brown will have those eggs for breakfast, Johnny!" Just then they heard Mrs. Brown.

"Breakfast is ready! Come and get it!" she called.

"Let's go, Johnny! I'm hungry! I know you and your daddy are hungry, too. Let's go eat!" They walked out of the chicken coop and Farmer Brown closed the door. "Over here, just inside the garage, is a place where we can all get washed up. It makes Mrs. Farmer Brown happy when I wash up good before I go in the house. Here's some soap and some clean towels. Let's hurry! I'm starving! I'm hungry enough to eat a horse!" Farmer Brown looked at Johnny, and saw that his eyes were big again. "Oh, no, Johnny. I couldn't eat a horse. I just mean to say that I am really hungry! I want some breakfast, and I know Mrs. Farmer Brown has a good one for us. Are you ready? Let's go!"

They headed for the house. Oh, it smelled so good! Mr. Farmer Brown opened the door and held it for Johnny and his daddy to go inside.

"My, my! If it isn't my friend Johnny and his daddy!" Mrs. Farmer Brown said. "You just come right on in here and sit down! I've fixed a breakfast fit for a king! But you and my Farmer Brown can eat it. Just as soon as we pray, you can dig right in! Go ahead, Farmer Brown."

Farmer Brown bowed his head. "Thank You, Heavenly Father, for this food. Thank You for Your goodness to us every day of our lives. Bless this food to the health of our bodies. Thank You for our good friends, Johnny and his daddy. Amen."

"Dig in!" Mrs. Farmer Brown said. "Help yourself! I fixed a big farmer breakfast for you, and I want you to enjoy every bite of it!"

Daddy put some food on Johnny's plate. The way Johnny chowed down told Daddy he really was hungry! They ate and talked, and talked and ate. Soon Daddy said, "Oh, I'm full! I can't eat another bite! How about you, Johnny? Have you had enough to eat?"

"My tummy's full, Daddy! Look how fat it is! " Johnny pushed his tummy out, and rubbed it. Farmer Brown and Mrs. Farmer Brown chuckled.

"We certainly do thank you for inviting us to visit your farm," Johnny's daddy said. "I've enjoyed it, and I know Johnny has, too. Thank you, Farmer Brown. And this breakfast was a smorgasbord, Mrs. Farmer Brown! Thank you very much!" Daddy got up from his chair. "I think we'd better be on our way now."

"Can we go see the piggies again, Daddy?" Johnny asked. "I like the piggies and the cows and the horsies and the chickens and the kitty cat. Can I watch Farmer Brown squirt the kitty with milk again, Daddy? I liked that."

Daddy picked Johnny up. "Not now, Johnny. Farmer Brown has work to do. And I know Mama has some work for me to do. We have to go, but we'll come back again sometime, okay?"

"Okay, Daddy. Will you ask us to come again, Farmer Brown? Will you let us watch you squirt milk in the kitty's mouth?"

"I sure will, Johnny," Farmer Brown said. "I sure will ask you to come and see us again."

"Mrs. Farmer Brown," Johnny said, "will you fix us a 'gusbord' again, like Daddy said?" Johnny couldn't say that big word.

Mrs. Farmer Brown laughed. "You betcha, I will, Johnny! I'll make a 'gusbord' breakfast just like I fixed for you today!"

Daddy and Johnny got in their car and went home. Johnny told Mama all about his trip to the farm. He was so excited! His eyes were so big! His words came so fast! Mama had a hard time putting it all together. But one thing she knew—Johnny liked the farm. That was plain to see.

* * *

Andy always sat very still as I whispered my made-up stories in his ear. He liked them all, but the Farmer Brown story was his favorite. He often asked me to tell him that story again, whether we were at the prison, or elsewhere. I would tell him again, the best I could remember. He always listened intently—guess I did it right!

LITTLE BROTHER, SCOTT

On September 10, 1987, Karen gave birth to Scott Preston. I spent a week at Karen's house to help when she came home from the hospital, as I did when Andy was born. Those were very special times for me.

It was that very weekend that the city was hosting its annual celebration. A parade was scheduled for Saturday afternoon, and we all decided to go. I held little Scott. He was so quiet and still—until he decided it was time to eat! He wanted the whole world to know that little baby Scott was hungry! And he did his best to announce it! This little guy had a mind of his own! There was no fussing before the dam broke loose! No, he went from quiet and calm, to screaming out at peak volume! As loud as he could! Right now! Nonstop! I've often told Karen that was an early peek at his personality, even when he was just a few days old.

TIME FOR CHANGE

In 1988, we moved into town. Clois and I both worked there. Sheila was a resident there, in the Skilled Nursing Facility of the Reed City Hospital. Our church was located there. We were always in town. So we decided it would be much easier if we lived there.

We had been living in our new home for only a couple of days, when the phone rang. It was Steve. He had just been transferred to a correctional facility half the distance of Jackson Prison, only eighty miles from us. "Mom, it's beautiful here, like a state park," he said, in a broken voice. "It's so good to see something besides cement," he continued to cry. "There are so many trees here."

I cried with him, and celebrated the fact that he was in a much-improved place, and that he was no longer one hundred fifty miles away, but only eighty. He filled me in on visiting hours, and I told him when we would be there.

Steve was still in prison, still incarcerated, but the move was good. We all appreciated it, and thanked God for yet another blessing on Steve's long journey—our journey, as well.

When Karen and Mark and the little boys came home, Andy and Scott visited Uncle Steve with the rest of us—until the guidelines changed. Somewhere along the journey, when the boys were about eleven and eight, their visits were no longer allowed. Since that rule change, the only children under eighteen allowed in the visiting room are the children, stepchildren, and grandchildren of an inmate.

So the boys and Uncle Steve haven't seen much of each other over the years. We have felt bad about that, but we were powerless to change anything. We knew time would take care of the problem, and it has. Andy has been able to visit for quite a while and, in just a few months, Scott will qualify for visits. Then their only restrictions will be distance and busy schedules, as they get involved in responsibilities in the adult world.

Each One Holds a Rosebud, Waiting For a Bloom

Another year passes. Another year is gone.
The calendar is changed. The year is history.
We're traveling along on a new stretch of time.
Where the road leads, we'll have to wait to see.

Near the entrance of the new year
Many people huddle just inside the door—
They seem to have something in common—
They are wondering what is in store.

Each one holds a rosebud stem,
Each one waits for a beautiful bloom.
On the archway overhead is a sign—
It says, "The Waiting Room."

Each person is waiting for something—
Some have waited for many a year
For a solution to end their problems,
For resolution of their fears.

Those who wait are of varied age—
From the young to the very old.
As I enter the room and express an interest
Their stories begin to unfold—

Ruth is waiting for restoration
Of relationship with her brother,
A sweet eight-year-old waits for adoption—
Hungering for love from a father and mother.

An attractive thirty-year-old lady
Is still waiting for her man—
A young couple longs for a baby—
She just miscarried again.

Tom has hope of walking someday—
He's determined, daily gives it a try.
Vera has been sickly for quite some time—
She prays, "Lord, is it time yet, for me to die?"

Jan is waiting for a friend—
"Just one good friend," she prays every day.
She has read that a lifetime may bring only one—
And even now, Jan is turning gray.

Brent is waiting for acceptance from Dad,
Bob is waiting for someone to care,
Lyndon is waiting for healing from grief—
He misses his companion, who is no longer there.

Each person in the room holds an unopened rose,
Each waits for a beautiful bloom.
Some of the rose stems stand tall, full of promise,
Some are wilted, held by the one in The Room.

Hope may diminish, as time goes by,
As some of the rosebuds declare.
And did you notice? Some hold more than one rosebud
    stem—
No one ever promised that life would be fair.

How long must one stay in The Waiting Room?
Many people have been there for years—
But life continues—they do what must be done—
When their eyes blur and they can't see, they stop and wipe
    their tears.

*My heartache is with me
every morning
when I awaken . . .
It doesn't go away.*

*My God doesn't go away either!
When I awaken
each morning,
He is here!*

Eight

THE "DAILY-NESS" OF LIFE

Morning after morning, year after year, we awaken to face the long-term tragedies of our second- and third-born—Sheila, still comatose after many years; and Steve's long-term incarceration, soon to be twenty years.

Steve's sentence was announced for all to hear. He would be out of circulation for a long time, imprisoned behind locked steel doors and razor wire fences, with multiple limitations and regulations. It was clearly spelled out. But Sheila's length of sentence isn't clear. There is no pronouncement of her future. Hers is a prison of a different nature. She is locked within herself, without means to vent her frustrations. It is probable that she has experienced stress in several parameters of her existence. Stress always takes its toll.

Occasionally Sheila blesses me with a smile. Once, in a great while, a faint sound of laughter comes from deep within her.

Infrequently through the years, Sheila exhibited briefly what appeared to be a slightly playful spirit. When that happened, I experimented at different times, attempting an interchange with her, only to realize she did not make appropriate responses to stimulation outside of her imprisoned world.

Sheila's facial expression sometimes communicates pain. Yes, my sweet Sheila is imprisoned in a different sense of the word. She is incarcerated within herself, and totally incapacitated.

Head injuries—even injuries much less severe than Sheila's—cause susceptibility to seizures. Sheila has had more than her share. Over the years, the nursing staff and all of us working together have learned to respond quickly to the slightest seizure activity. This quick response has helped immensely in controlling her seizures. Sometimes simply providing peaceful, quiet surroundings and decreasing the light in the room, relieves Sheila of the problem. On other occasions, medication is required.

Pneumonia is a continual threat to Sheila's well being. Her long-term abdominal feeding tube has created its own set of complications. In May 2001, Sheila was very ill with all of these, including congestive heart failure. We thought for sure we were going to lose her, as we watched her struggle for every breath. We thought she was going home to be with Jesus, but for some reason He didn't take her. She amazingly recovered and was back to her "normal."

Why do You leave Sheila here, Lord Jesus?

She has been lying here for so long!

Why doesn't God take her, after all these years of being totally incapacitated? Of course, there was no answer for my question, and no place to carry out research that would provide an answer. It was beyond the earthly realm. There was no way of knowing Sheila's "length of sentence."

Many things I did not know, but these things I knew—

Peace in coping with Sheila's injury comes only in trusting God, in knowing and believing He loves her, in knowing He is taking care of her, and in recognizing Him as The Sovereign God.

Peace comes in knowing God is in control, in knowing His ways are above my ways, in believing He sees the pretty patterned side of the quilt, as well as the back. He sees the future, the whole picture. I see only the mass of tangled threads on the back, the "now" situations we live with.

Peace in Steve's situation comes through making the same applications—knowing God is in control, and trusting Him. It is a priceless comfort to me, to know Steve has placed his trust in God. That fact elicits praise to God from my heart! Without that knowledge I would have great difficulty in coping with his life situation.

STEVE

Many Mom-questions run round and round in my mind regarding Steve's future. When will he be released? Will he marry someday? Will he be allowed to establish a fairly normal life on the outside? How will he make a living? Health concerns—heart problems run rampant in his dad's family. Dental concerns—his teeth have not been cared for during his years of imprisonment. Will he find a church that will accept him? Will he find a place of ministry, a place to serve? When he is released, how will he manage life on the outside, facing decisions, when most of his decisions have been made for him for the majority of his adult life? Will he be equipped and able to cope with all the changes in our world that have passed him by? On and on the questions go. I must surrender them all to God . . .

GOD, YOU REALLY DESIRE MY PRAISE?

In previous chapters I wrote how God had gently encouraged me to praise Him. So gently, yet so clearly—leaving no doubt, God impressed upon me that my praise would please Him; that He desired my praise! Reflecting on those earlier days of God's ministry, I wonder, Why did God want me to praise Him? Why would He desire my praise? Why does God desire my praise today? It is awesome to think the God of creation, the God of the universe, even cares about me! He really cares about what is happening in my life! But He is the Author of Everything! Why is praise from this simple, unknown, heartbroken mother something God, in all of His greatness, desires?

At the time of Sheila's accident I was so burdened with sorrow, so devastated, I didn't ask many questions. I was desperate for one drop of strength, desperate for something to cling to. I held tightly to any tiny grain of hope God gave me, through His Word, from the speaker behind the pulpit, in prayer, from Christian radio—I held on for dear life. If God wanted my praise—Yes! I would praise Him! No questions asked.

Receiving and accepting God's personal nudging, I began my walk down the Pathway of Praise. Concurrently, but without me being aware of this truth, I began my slow, unsteady walk down the Pathway of Healing. Please note the word "began". My heartache was no less. Down on all fours, beside my bed, I cried out to God, sometimes until I was weak and nearly collapsed, while I poured out my heart to Him.

Continuing my journey on the Pathway of Praise has been the steadying force in my sorrow. Giving praise to God and maintaining a heart attitude of praise, has been my strengthening, my keeping power, my peace. It has been my victory, in the face of heartbreaking loss.

After Steve's arrest, I took a fork in the road. Rather than continuing on the Pathway of Praise, I turned down a road I'll call "Heartbreak Highway." My eyes were glued to our ugly and hopeless circumstances. I had tunnel vision. God, in His wisdom and knowledge of all things, allowed me some grieving time. Then, one day, He gently called to me again and confronted me with His question, "Don't you think it's time to praise Me?"

"You are right, Lord," I agreed. "It is time to praise You!" His question was very gentle. He understood my aching heart. But the truth of His question jolted me from where I was on Heartbreak Highway, to where He wanted me to be—trusting Him, and looking to Him for strength, while I traveled the Pathway of Praise! So I began praising Him! Publicly I praised Him the following Sunday evening during testimony time.

A VERSE THAT SPEAKS MY HEART

I need a life verse, I thought. I hear other people quote a verse they have claimed as their own, but I don't have one. I have never given it much consideration, but I think it would be good to select one to declare as my own foundational verse. I'm going to search scripture until I find a verse that speaks my heart.

I began my search. The timeline was about twenty years into Sheila's injury. Throughout those twenty years I experienced God's loving ministry, from the first intense emotions of my broken heart, to the place of accepting and pouring my love into my totally incapacitated Sheila—day after day, month after month, year after year. God prompted my spirit through His ministry, to know that He is my Everything! He is Everything I need!

I searched. How could I choose one verse out of all the marvelous verses in scripture? Quite some time later, I made my selection. *"If your law had not been my delight, I would have perished in my affliction."* (Psalm 119:92 NIV)

"That's the one, Lord. That is so true! If I had not turned to You— first of all for forgiveness and salvation; secondly in my sorrow, I

would be without hope! I would be a sour, dried up, prune-of-a-woman. I would be weighed down with heaviness, depression, and hopelessness. I would have perished, even though my heart was beating. But You provide hope for me! Thank You, Jesus!"

With God's inspiration to praise Him in the early days of my sorrow, a close runner-up for my life verse(s) was Psalm 104:33-34: *"I will sing unto the Lord as long as I live: I will sing praise to my God while I have my being. My meditation of him shall be sweet: I will be glad in the Lord."* But Psalm 119:92 just seems to say it all very concisely. I'm content with my choice.

RECOMMENDATION

Whatever life hands you, I recommend praising God. I know from experience, it isn't always easy. It may take some time to get to the place where you can do it. Tragedy isn't handled easily, quickly, or lightly. It's a heavy, heavy load. Time is required to work through the tough stuff of life. How well I know that! But I will ever be thankful that early on in our tragedies God made known to me, that my praise was what He desired. I am also thankful for His involvement in my heart before that time. I am thankful that when He came to me with that request, I was prepared to respond in the affirmative. My healing was accomplished more quickly and more completely, because I said yes to God's expression of desire for my praise.

Are there still hurts regarding Sheila and Steve? Yes. There always will be. I still have days when their situations seem more than I can handle. I have to bow before the Lord in prayer. *"Dear Jesus, please take this hurt. It is so deep, so overwhelming. I'm weak today, and I can't handle it, Lord. I give it to You, and ask for Your strength to carry me."*

As Mom, I have concerns that cut deeply into the depths of my being. (Some of my concerns never enter Dad's mind. I understand that to be simply the difference between the thinking pattern of male and female. I will never, ever believe the only difference in men and women is anatomy!) I must place all of my concerns in the capable hands of my Heavenly Father. There is nothing I can do about them! Nothing! I have to trust Him. So I will continue to praise Him. He has been faithful in the past. He will be faithful today. *"Praise to You, Faithful Father God!"*

God's personal and very precious ministry after Sheila's injury helped prepare me for the devastation of Steve's crime, his consequent arrest, and imprisonment. God's ministry at that time strengthened my heart to trust Him, and lean hard on Him. It equipped me with a deeper faith and a fortifying solidarity, as I struggled in the intensity of my pain for Steve. The hurt was no less. The heartache was not erased. But, because of my enriched faith, I was much better prepared. When I came through the dark tunnel, God was there to welcome me with open arms of love. He had been there all the time. I just couldn't see Him through the dark shadows of my sorrow.

Oh, Pretty Butterfly

Oh, Pretty Butterfly, as you fly through the air
You're on top of the world without ever a care.
Oh, Pretty Butterfly! Just to be like you—
To be without problems! What I wouldn't do!

I know—you were a caterpillar, you were bound
To crawling on objects, or crawling on the ground
By the limits placed upon you, never soaring through the air.
Your colors were dull and drab, no pretty colors there.

But you have changed, Pretty Butterfly—
You're graceful and beautiful, as you flutter by!
Your travel is effortless and free
As I watch you flit and flutter close by me.

You land and I see something I haven't seen before.
You fold your wings as if in prayer, before you fly on more.
Do Pretty Butterflies pray? I really have much doubt,
But that's what I'm pretending, as I see you flit about—

That you stop on your journey to take time for a rest,
And fold your wings in prayer before continuing on your quest.
Oh, Pretty Butterfly, watching you there on the tree,
I see in you a clear message for me.

I need often, on my journey of life
As mother, sister, neighbor, friend, and wife,
To take time to fold my hands in prayer,
To seek God's guidance for my every need and care.

The needs of my family, my husband, my kids,
Prayer for their future, the situation in their midst,
For their health, and love, their education, and all—
My Father in heaven, yes, on Him I must call.

I must offer words of gratitude to God, and give Him praise
For daily blessings, and strength for all my days.
Oh, Pretty Butterfly, before you fly away,
Thank you for the lesson you have given me today.

Nine

Prayer

"Pastor, how should we pray for Sheila? Should we demand her healing? Should we just pray, 'Take care of Sheila, Lord. May Your will be done'? How should we pray?" Three days had passed since Sheila's injury. We sat in the hospital coffee shop with our pastor and his wife. There had been no change in Sheila's condition—still classified as grave.

Of course, we had been praying for Sheila. Each morning my husband and I prayed together, asking God to take care of her. We prayed for ourselves, asking God for strength to face whatever the day brought. We needed help! We needed Him! The load of sorrow was heavy!

As we sat there, with our pastor and his wife, I approached him with my question, "Pastor, how should we pray for Sheila?"

"I don't believe we can or should demand God's healing," Pastor said. "You see, God is a God of Love. He sees the whole picture. He sees Sheila. He knows all about her. He sees you, and

He sees your broken hearts. He hears you as you pray. He hears even more than the words you say. He hears the deep cries of your heart. He knows your thoughts. He knows you love Sheila. I think God is saying, 'My Dear Children, you just keep pouring your hearts out to me, and trust Me. I know what is happening. I see the whole picture. I love Sheila and I love you. Trust Me. Just trust Me.'"

Overwhelmed with sorrow, we needed input from our spiritual leader—wise counsel and guidance. Our pastor's comments were comforting to us. We appreciated his words.

Time went on, and I continued to pour out my heart to God. There were no answers anywhere! No answers at all! Just wait! Keep trusting God. There were only two choices—either turn my back on God and say, "Forget God! Believing in Him makes no difference in this situation." Or trust Him. I chose to keep trusting Him in the darkness, and in the waiting.

With the passing of time, and after I had prayed more prayers for Sheila than I could count, I began to see a change—not in Sheila, but in myself. God was working in my heart. He was giving me insight on the depths of His love. He was helping me see that His heart ached for us, His children. He was showing me that when we hurt, He hurt. I understood that He loved Sheila even more than I did—a greater love than I could even imagine.

Through praying, reading scripture, and God's personal ministry, my faith increased. I knew the only way to pray for Sheila was to pour out my heart to God, place her in His care, and leave the rest up to Him. I knew His ways were greater than our ways. (Isaiah 55:8-9)

DISAPPOINTMENT WITH GOD

It was the fall of 1974. We were doing well as a family. Our church and associated activities were a very important part of our lives. Through the years I had been doing the right things, as wife and mother. I had read scripture and prayed with the kids before they left for school most mornings. Dad left for work early, so on weekdays it was up to me.

The music we enjoyed in our home was that which lifted up the name of Jesus. We had a wonderful record of dramatized Bible stories, which our children listened to over and over . . . and over. They loved repetition, and they loved these stories!

With few exceptions, we attended every service in our church as a family of two. As we grew into a family of five we continued to follow that pattern. Yes, I had done the right things—the best I knew—in living the Christian life. Clois and I had done the best we knew in training our children in spiritual pathways. Yet, I was disappointed in my own relationship with the Lord. It seemed that it made very little difference in our lives that we were Christians—if it made any difference at all. Things seemed to go along day after day, just about the same as with our neighbors, many who made no claim to be Christian. I was disappointed, expecting and wanting more in my relationship with Jesus.

So I prayed: *"Lord, I'm disappointed. I was expecting more from the Christian life. I'm not sure what, but I was looking for more, a closer walk with You, Lord. Our lives don't seem any different than those of others around us, who don't claim to know You. Shouldn't life be different for people who love You, God?"*

I thought about this picture, and reasoned, I think what I need is a miracle. If God would send me something from out of the blue, with no explanation, I'm sure that would help me. I would know God really is involved in our lives. I would know He does make a difference! Yes, I need a miracle—something specific. What shall I ask God for? For several days I considered the options, the various requests I could make, in the way of a miracle. Finally I decided what it would be.

So I prayed again: *"Lord, Karen is going to graduate from high* school in the spring. I don't need to tell You that. You already know. We'll be having an open house to celebrate her accomplishment. You know what our davenport looks like, Lord. It's ugly. It's old and brown. Yes, I know it's useable. It doesn't have any holes in it, but it is ugly, Lord. If You would send us a new one, or at least a pretty one, from somewhere out of the blue, I would know it was a miracle from You! I would know You are involved in our lives!"

Up until this time, life had been good. We were a happy, intact family. We were comfortable. Our marriage was a happy one. Our home was peaceful. But, oh, how naïve I was in those days! My prayer revealed my naiveté, believing something tangible would meet my need. The miracle of a davenport from an unknown source would not have done much for any of us. It would not have impacted me or any of us for long. No way would it have been a life-changing event.

God, in His infinite wisdom and love, understood the real cry of my heart, when I expressed my need in that naïve request. He answered that heart cry—a prayer for more of Him. He answered in His way and in His perfect timing. He knew what was ahead, not far down the road of life. He knew I would have a very real need when that time came—not just a desire for a prettier davenport.

God's personal ministry to me after Sheila's accident was the answer to my prayer! I am convinced of that! His ministry since that time, has, indeed, been life changing! Today I know God makes a difference in my life, and in the life of each member of my family!

PRAYERS FOR SHEILA

"Lord, please heal Sheila's sore lip. It hurts her so, Lord. It's just a minor thing, compared to her injury, but it pains her. Would you take away that little hurt, Lord?"

It seems the Lord has had a deaf ear to my prayers for Sheila since her accident—prayers regarding her healing and relief from pain. I'm not complaining, just acknowledging, as I see it, that God has chosen not to answer my prayers, as I have stated them, for Sheila. Through the years I have talked to Him, more times than I can number, about a multitude of concerns—seizures, painful and oft-returning canker sores, flushed face, tearing and painful red eyes. I have expressed concern in prayer about her caregivers—some excellent, and others just putting in their time.

Perhaps God did answer some of my less specific prayers, and I didn't recognize His answers. But whether He answered them or not, this one thing I know—God, with His heart of love, in all of His mercy and grace, has been involved through the years in all that has gone on in Sheila's life, and in our lives. I thank Him, and praise Him for His Presence! I praise Him for His inter-working in the whole picture! *"God you are trustworthy! You are faithful! You are in control! Praise Your Holy Name!"*

STEVE—NOW THAT'S ANOTHER STORY!

Does God still perform miracles? "Yes! Yes! He does!" That's my answer! Time after time I have seen God's hand in Steve's life, providing just what he needed at just the right time. Some of the problems he has faced flash through my mind, even as I write. I remember his concern, and ours. There was nothing we could do to fix these matters—nothing we could do except lay everything out before God. He has blessed Steve and us with one miracle, and then another—GOD-GIVEN!

Reviewing these events, I am humbled again, and ever so thankful. I bow my head and say, *"Thank You, Lord! Thank You! You are trustworthy! You have proven that time and time again! Thank You!"*

HOOKED ON NICOTINE

Steve stopped smoking cold turkey. He had never smoked when he was home, but when he was in the county jail before his sentencing, a friend who smoked gave him money for cigarettes—thinking, I presume, that smoking would be a help and comfort to him. So Steve began to smoke, and he was hooked. He smoked for several years before the health issues became a serious concern to him. Then he began to feel that smoking wasn't pleasing to God. He tried to quit, but struggled with it for a long time. Then, one day, God revealed to Steve just a snippet of the ugliness of smoking. Steve quit. Cold turkey! He was done!

"Thank You, Lord! Thank You for giving Steve strength to quit smoking on the spot! I praise You, Holy Father!"

A GOD-THING!

When I pray, I come before God with what I consider to be a "need." God weighs my wants and my needs. I don't always see the difference between the two, but He does. His promise is to meet our NEEDS. I had reminded God of Steve's situation, his need. I prayed that He would rearrange schedules, and make changes, so Steve could attend church services. God didn't do what I asked of Him. He did something better!

"I have something to tell you, Mom and Dad," Steve said one day, as soon as we greeted him in the visiting room. "But I'll wait until you're done shopping, Mom, so I can tell you both at once."

I finished my "shopping." What marvelous shopping opportunities in the prison visiting room! Vending machines! I selected a sandwich for Steve—better to shop early, while there is at least a little variety available. I was anxious to hear what Steve had to say. He was fairly bursting to share it.

"I have a Christian roommate now. His name is Tom. You've

seen him out on visits before. I'll point him out to you when he comes in. He's a good Christian guy."

Steve told us this move was totally unexpected. Tom was alone in a room after his "bunkie" left. He didn't want a smoker to move in with him. He mentioned to guards that Bowman had a bunkie that smoked, and Bowman didn't smoke. That was all it took! Officials approved the move, and Tom moved in!

"You should see Tom's books!" Steve said enthusiastically. "He has more than I do! He likes to study scripture, too. Some of his books look very interesting. Since Tom moved in, we've been praying together at lock-down time."

"Lord," I prayed. *"My prayer was for Steve to be allowed to attend services, to worship and fellowship with the guys. This isn't an answer to my prayer."* I was disheartened, but I didn't let Steve see my disappointment.

A couple of days later, the light dawned. *"Lord, You did answer my prayer! But You answered more abundantly! Thank You, Lord! Thank You, Holy Father! You have proven Yourself again! I can trust You!"*

What an unexpected blessing and surprise it was for Steve—for us, too! I realized personally the truth of scripture. No way can I match, outdo, or out-think the Lord! " . . . *I am come that they might have life, and that they might have it more abundantly."* (John 10:10)

"Thank You, Father God, for answering my prayer in a greater measure than I ever dreamed. I had prayed You would make it possible for Steve to attend church services. I prayed You might change his work schedule so he would be available at service time. He really missed fellowship with the Christian guys, and I thought he needed that. Holy Father, You, in all Your wisdom and knowledge, gave him a Christian roommate—someone he can fellowship with every day! A roommate to pray with every day during count time! Your answer was much better than I could even imagine to request!

Thank You, Holy Father! You are Faithful! You are Incredible! I can count on You!"

DOUBLE-BUNK? NO!

"The whole place is going to be double-bunked by 1990. That's the rumor," Steve told us. It was mid-1989. This information was very upsetting to me. It meant there would be two men housed in a room built for one man—very close quarters. That was a real concern for Mom, with all the issues presented in prison life. One worrisome issue is homosexuality, ever present. Television is a worry. Headsets are usually available, but they wear out or break, and are not always replaced. What if Steve's bunkie wants to watch something evil, and doesn't use his headset? Even if he does use them, the screen is right there, "in your face," in such a small room. I talked to the Lord about those concerns. I asked Him to intervene and protect Steve from double-bunking. The rumor said "all would be double-bunked," but I knew there was a way. There are always exceptions. And I knew God's resources are unlimited.

As the rumored deadline closed in, we visited Steve one day on our normal schedule. "Well, Mom and Dad, I'm double-bunked now." My heart sank. Inwardly I cried, *"Lord, that was not a selfish prayer on my part! You know my concerns are legitimate! The concerns I expressed to You are Your concerns also, from what I read in Your Word!"*

I hit bottom! God had let me down! Why should I pray? It didn't change anything. My request was very reasonable. My concerns were God's concerns also. My prayer made no difference! Why bother to pray?

Disappointment owned my heart and my emotions. The hurt was real and it was heavy. For a month I couldn't pray. I didn't pray. But God was patient with me, while I worked through my despair. I reviewed past experiences with God. I knew Him to be a God of love; faithful and trustworthy. Ever so slowly I began to come up out of that sludge pit. I began to understand that living in such close quarters would challenge Steve. This could be a real learning experience for him. Perhaps God had placed Steve in this "special training school" for a while. Finally, I reached the top of that pit of disappointment, and climbed out. At last I gained victory over the darkness, and I began to pray again.

After double bunking was established, Steve had various roommates through the years—smokers, vulgar guys, men with very different religious beliefs. Now and then Steve was blessed to have a Christian roommate. The constant transfer of guys to other correctional facilities, guys going home, and new guys coming in continually, brings about a frequent change in room partners. It happens with only a few hours notice: "You are 'riding out' tomorrow. Be packed and ready to go after breakfast in the morning." Inmates are seldom told where they are going and they have little time to say "Farewell, my good friend," to Christian brothers, with whom deep relationships have been established.

HE "RODE OUT"

It was Friday. June 6, 2004. Keeping our regular schedule, we traveled the eighty miles to visit Steve. We registered for our visit, then sat down until Steve was contacted and ready. In twenty minutes our names were called. Steve was up. We entered the "bubble" area, where we would be frisked, after walking through the metal detector. (Hopefully it wouldn't beep. If it did, the "guilty" one began a process of elimination, until they could walk through without eliciting a beep. A handheld detector is sometimes employed in that process.) As the male guard frisked Clois, he said, "Steve isn't happy today. His bunkie rode out this morning."

"Oh, Tom's gone?" Clois responded.

"Yup. He left this morning after breakfast."

By that time we were approved to enter the visiting room. Our IDs and coins had been checked. We each had been given an orange VISITOR tag, and had clipped it to our shoulder area. The guard in the "bubble" opened the electric doors so we could proceed to the visiting room.

When we saw Steve, we knew the guard was right. Steve wasn't happy. He proceeded to tell us what happened. Tom had been informed Thursday evening that he was being transferred on Friday; told to be packed and ready to go in the morning. Friday morning Steve went to work in the kitchen at 5:30 a.m. He saw Tom at breakfast. When Steve completed his day's work at 1:30, Tom was gone, destination unknown.

Steve was concerned about Tom and about himself. What facility was Tom transferred to? His fiancée, who lived nearby, visited him often. Was she going to have a long drive to visit him now? Who would Tom have for a bunkie? Who would Steve have for a bunkie? This was a heavy concern for each of them, and for us.

After three hours of talking and snacking with Steve, we rose from our seats to leave. We told him we would pray that God would be involved in his concerns regarding a new roommate; that God would send him a compatible guy—and even better, a Christian guy for a bunkie. That would be an extra blessing!

Clois and I went to the One who knows all things, to the One who has unlimited resources. We laid out these needs before Him.

A GOD-THING, INDEED!

A week later when we visited Steve, he told us he had a new bunkie when he returned to his room after our visit that Friday—a young guy who seemed to be compatible, but he wasn't a Christian. On Monday the young guy, who had been at the facility before, was out in the prison yard. A guard recognized him, remembered where he had been housed before, and asked if he would like to go back to that unit, where he would know some guys. The young man said yes, he would like to do that. So it happened. He was moved back to his former unit. He took the bed of an inmate by the name of Gary, who, in turn, moved into Steve's room to occupy the empty bed there. Gary is a Christian! Miraculous details are involved, in bringing Gary into Steve's room! Listen in on their conversation, as Gary moves his footlocker and few possessions into Steve's room . . .

"Hey, my name's Steve. Welcome! Make yourself as comfortable as possible. You know how that goes. We have our limits." Steve stuck out his hand for a handshake.

"Name's Gary. Thanks for the welcome; doesn't happen often, ya know."

"Did you ride in today?" Steve asked.

"No, I've been here about three weeks; moved into Alpine in Unit Four. But early this morning I was told to pack up. 'You're going to a different unit,' the guard said. So about ten o'clock a young guy appears at my door with Captain Benson. The guy has his gear with him, and he's moving into my room. I guess the guy lived in Alpine before when he was in this facility. Someone told me a guard recognized him when he was out in the yard, and asked if he would like to move in with some guys he knew."

"Sounds like the young guy that just left here," Steve said. "He moved in with me on Friday. I didn't have time to get acquainted with him. Where did you ride in from, Gary?"

"Came from Cottonville," Gary said, as he arranged his belongings on his desk.

"Hey, my friend Sam is there. In fact, Sam—hey, do you know Sam Wheaton?"

"Do I know Sam Wheaton?" Gary turned from his desk and

looked at Steve. "Sure I do! Sam is a good friend of mine!" Gary responded enthusiastically.

"So . . . " Steve spoke slowly, as he began to put things together. "Gary, you must be the one Sam wrote to me about a few weeks ago!" Steve's voice grew louder as he realized what had just happened. "Sam said his friend Gary had recently transferred here. He told me to watch for you. He said you are a Christian, and you are interested in learning more about scripture and the Christian life." Steve looked at Gary in amazement!

Gary stood, statue-like, by his desk in the small room. Wonder was written all over his face. He shook his head. "I can't believe this! Out of all the guys in this facility . . . I end up here, in this room, as your bunkie! I can't believe it! Sam told me about you—his good friend, Steve. He told me he roomed with you when he was in this facility. This is unbelievable!"

"There's only one explanation for it, Gary. God did it! It's a God-thing!"

"Wow!" Gary agreed. "You're right, Steve! This has to be a God-thing! Wait until Sam hears about this!"

"Holy Father, how can this Mom thank You sufficiently? How can I ever doubt Your intimate involvement in the lives of Your people? Your Word says in Matthew 10:29, 'Are not two sparrows sold for a farthing? and one of them shall not fall on the ground without your Father.' Steve, according to this world's standards, is a sparrow. He doesn't have much value. He's in prison serving time, paying for what he did—living under the lock-the-door-and-throw-away-the-key attitude of many of this world. But he is one of Your children. I know You take care of Your children! Praise Your Holy Name, Father! Thank You! Thank You!"

Ten

DEAR GOD, PLEASE GLORIFY YOURSELF

oly Father, I pray You will work in Sheila's suffering and our hurting. I pray this will not all be in vain, but that somehow You will receive glory. I pray You will work in the whole situation, and bring about good in this tragedy that has come to Sheila, and brought heartache to us." (Should we label it that way? *Tragedy*? I wonder . . .)

"We didn't want or ask for this situation, Lord. But here we are in the midst of Sheila's incapacitating injury. Our sweet, vivacious, and outgoing daughter lies quiet and still on the hospital bed—totally helpless, incapacitated. She can't walk. She can't talk. She can't communicate in any way. Holy Father God, please be in charge of this situation. I pray You will receive praise and honor through it all. May Your kingdom be increased through this heartache, Dear Lord. Amen."

This was the prayer of my heart. Again and again I laid my

desire out before God. This heartache we found ourselves in, and Sheila's extensive injury, was far too costly to be wasted.

"Lord, please work in this. Please bring glory to Yourself, and increase Your kingdom through our heartache, through Sheila's injury. May Your name be praised!"

"LORD, YOU ARE ASKING ME TO SPEAK FOR YOU?"

I am a quiet person who prefers to stay in the background—not a speaker. Occasionally I come out of my shell and do something unpredictable, but that is only occasionally, and in a specific setting.

One day in the fall of 1978 . . .

"Lord, the thought that just streaked through my mind—what was that all about? Me? A speaker?" The thought was a flash in the pan, here and gone. There was no way I was prepared to do any speaking, to anybody, anywhere, at that time.

We weren't far down the road of Sheila's injury. It had changed her life, and ours, so drastically. I had not yet been through God's "training school." I had not yet experienced His tender love and patience. I didn't yet understand how He comes alongside His children; how He sometimes carries His children through the hard times. I had heard about His wonderful attributes, yes, but up to this point in my life it was mostly hearsay. It was something I had read about, or heard a saint speak about. It was not yet mine. No way was I ready to "speak" for God!

God's timing doesn't follow a clock or a calendar. We live with time zones—Atlantic, Eastern, Central, Mountain, Pacific—but God works in His time zone. He develops His people, according to His schedule.

Contemplating that fleeting thought about speaking for God, I recognize now that it was simply a tiny seed God planted in my heart. At that time I was wrapped up in survival, living with a broken heart, barely able to get one foot ahead of the other. No way was I ready, or able, to be involved in a speaking ministry. In His wisdom, God knew that. He had simply planted a seed . . .

On day two of Sheila's injury I began to keep notes. The Lord planted the desire within me. At that time I wrote of Sheila's condition and my Mom-feelings. It was the beginning of my dedication to journaling.

God continued His tender ministry to me for a year and a half following Sheila's injury. Yes, He continues His ministry to me even today. But during that time He built up my trust in Him. My faith was "ground level," and He worked in me to bolster it up, until it became established and had a solid foundation. During that time He taught me through His unlimited resources—through songs, sermons, Christian radio, autobiographies, and biographies. His Spirit prompted my spirit, as I read and studied His Word—and I wrote it in my journal.

Over the years, I have realized the value of my journal keeping. Because I wrote, I have an accurate account of my feelings and a record of Sheila's day-to-day condition. Reviewing my journal, I feel again the intensity of my heartache in those early days and months of her injury. My journal is a source of information, from which I can share God's tender ministry to my broken heart.

THE TIME HAS COME

One day, thirteen years after the surprising thought flashed through my mind about speaking for God, He communicated with my spirit that the time had come. "It's time now, time to speak for Me."

I was ready. *"Okay, Lord, the answer is yes. We have prayed that You would receive glory through Sheila's injury. If You say it's time, then it is time. If You want me to share what You have done in my heart and life I will do it, with Your help. You have prepared me! You have taught me! You have encouraged me! Knowing You have called me gives me purpose and strength. You lead the way, and I will follow! Thank You, Holy Father!"*

In the following weeks I took a few simple steps to make myself available. I created a promotional flyer, and ordered a conservative number from a printer. The owner/editor of a Christian newspaper, for which I had been writing, placed a ministry card in his paper for me.

Requests began to come in for me to speak at banquets, Christmas teas, Sunday school classes, senior citizen groups—a variety of gatherings. After three years of speaking at such one-time events, I spoke at a three-hundred-plus ladies' retreat, for the three main sessions. Other retreats followed, with each of these resulting in return invitations.

I kept plenty busy with everything on my plate—full-time employment, Sheila to watch over, Steve to visit weekly, Clois to love and feed (and pamper), a home to care for, keeping connected with Karen and her family, involvement in church, and speaking engagements.

When the Christian newspaper for which I was writing was discontinued in 2000, invitations began to taper off. My name was no longer visible. About that same time, I began to feel God was letting up on His desire that I speak for Him. I had peace and contentment, knowing I had been obedient to His will.

It looked like the speaking era of my life was drawing to a close. Perhaps God was going to take me to another avenue of service. Occasional proposals continued to trickle in, and they still do today. When possible, I fulfill those requests, but I don't have the God-given drive I had for the several years I was busy in that ministry.

God nurtured the seed He had planted in me, until it was in full bloom. He enabled me for a ministry that is almost totally out of character for me—so out of character that my husband was shocked when I told him God had called me to do it.

"This is love for God: to obey his commands. And his commands are not burdensome . . . " (I John 5:3 NIV)

"Thank You, God! May Your name be glorified!"

Eleven

PEOPLE . . . AND PEACE

"Lord, people make comments that sound so holy, so authoritarian, so 'in the know,' as if they have life and their relationship with You all figured out. Well, I don't, Lord. I'm just going to trust You. I hear what people say, but I'm just going to trust You."

GOD KNEW YOU COULD HANDLE THIS

"A tree is developed to the point of great strength because of the storms and hard winds it has endured. Storms force the tree to deepen its roots. That makes it a strong tree. God knew you could handle this tragedy of your daughter's injury. That's why He chose You. That's why He gave it to you."

I rejected this comment from an acquaintance. Portions of it may be true, but I chose to let it go. If God saw us as people of strong faith, wonderful. Should it be true, it isn't something to boast about.

Did God hover over earth and look for a young woman He wanted to burden with a debilitating head injury? Did He look down on Sheila, and say, "I'll inflict this injury on Sheila Bowman. She can take it"?

Did He look down on us, and say, "I see Clois and Bev Bowman down there on earth. They live in a little town in central Michigan. Their hearts are going to break today, but they can handle it"? No, I don't believe God operates that way.

THE RIGHT KIND OF FAITH, AND THE RIGHT AMOUNT

During conversations with people, the question of healing was often brought up. There were those who claimed the *right* amount of the right *kind* of faith would bring about Sheila's healing. I struggled with this. What is the *right* amount of faith, and the right *kind* of faith? Weeks and months went by, and Sheila remained the same. As I studied scripture and prayed, I understood the only way for me to pray was, *"Lord, may Your will be done. You know our hearts. You know how much we love our sweet Sheila. You know our hearts' desire is for her to be healed and restored to the sweetheart she was. If You choose to heal her, we will forever be grateful. But we surrender the whole situation to You. We place her in Your hands and trust her to Your care."* With that understanding, and giving up the struggle over the right kind and right amount of faith, I found a measure of peace.

Clois and I listened to quoted scripture verses. We listened as some offered what they considered to be the answer for our situation. We appreciated the expressions of concern and encouragement, the hugs and hand-on-the-shoulder approaches. We understood the words spoken were an effort to help our heartache, so we listened . . . held onto encouraging words, and chose to let many fall by the wayside . . .

A notable measure of peace came in surrendering to Jesus what Sheila had been, and accepting her as each day found her.

Oh yes, I wanted my Sheila back. How much I wanted her back! But she wasn't there anymore. Sheila had always been full of smiles. She shared them with everyone. Her smiles were gone. Sheila, as we had known her for almost nineteen years, wasn't there anymore! I began to slowly surrender her as she had been, and accept her as she was. I slowly loosened my grip on the hope each day, that I would see signs of the Sheila I had loved and known. I chose, rather, to see her as she was each day. Then, if I saw signs of her restoration, I would celebrate, and be encouraged to look for more.

This surrender provided a great measure of peace. It wasn't *"Okay, God. You are bigger than I am. You win."* It wasn't defiant or a defeatist surrender. It was more like this: *"God, You are in control. If I had my choice, Sheila would still be healthy, beautiful, and vivacious. But I have found You to be a God of love. I believe You are trustworthy and holy, and You know what You are doing. I trust You, Holy Father."*

The radiologist in the x-ray department where Sheila had been employed had great respect for her. He said, "When I came to work in the morning, I didn't have to step lightly until I knew what Sheila's mood was for the day. She was always the same. She knew what she believed, and was firm in it." Many times I saw tears in the doctor's eyes, as he visited Sheila in the extended care unit, and when he spoke of her.

Seeing and hearing of the love people had for Sheila always blessed us. They commented on her ready smile, her strong Christian beliefs, and her friendliness. Many recounted Sheila's simple acts of kindness and her concern for their comfort and welfare. When people affirmed the precious girl Sheila was, we appreciated it more than words could express.

"Holy Father, work in my heart. Mold, shape, and change me into the person You designed me to be. Teach me from Your Word, and from Your unlimited resources. Help me keep my eyes focused

on You, in this world that would influence me to follow the bright lights and the idols it places on pedestals. Teach me to be still when I should, and move when it's moving time, according to Your time frame. You have been faithful, Lord, and You will be faithful in the future. You can be no other way. You are God! Thank You, Holy Father. Amen."

Twelve

A LONG JOURNEY, INDEED

After Sheila passed the crisis of her injury, she was transferred to a long-term care facility in Grand Rapids, Michigan. Observing her care there, day after day, I was confident she could eventually be cared for in a facility nearer to our home. The constant travel and separation was hard on all of us. Steve was fifteen years old. He needed some stability and he needed to be with us. Clois had returned to work. We felt we needed to make a change.

On June 8, 1978, Sheila was transferred to a skilled nursing facility only ten miles from our home. This facility was a part of our local hospital, housed on the north end of the building complex.

Sheila was coming home. At the time of her accident Sheila had been employed in the Radiology Department of the hospital. A huge sign reading "Welcome Home, Sheila" greeted her, as the ambulance personnel rolled her into the extended care unit on a gurney.

Our days were full, occupied with all the usual, unending home responsibilities; Dad's work, teenager Steve, and caring for Sheila. Despite our busyness, during the next several months I was driven to spend time in scripture and prayer. It was an absolute necessity. It was my means of survival.

We were closely involved in Sheila's treatment, watching over her, and watching out for her. We were her mouthpiece, doing our best to see that she was well cared for and comfortable.

Various methods of stimulation were employed in hopes of eliciting a response from Sheila and, ultimately, arousal from her comatose state. The greatest response we ever saw was a slight effort to turn her head toward Clois when he spoke her name. That thrilled us. But Sheila never progressed. We watched her struggle to turn slightly toward Dad a few times, over a few months. It seemed to take every ounce of concentration within her just to make that tiny movement. After those few months, we continued to watch, but Sheila showed no more response.

Twenty-two months after Sheila's transfer, I took a part-time job at the hospital. I felt it would be easier on me. I could check on Sheila often. If I were needed in an emergency I would be available. It would help us financially, too.

Days, months, and years passed. Sheila remained bedridden. She didn't move. She didn't talk. She did nothing voluntarily. She lay as she was placed, until she was repositioned two hours later.

I told Sheila often that I loved her. I told her she was beautiful. I knew many people wondered how I could see beauty in her. They couldn't see it. They would be repulsed by her sometimes drooling mouth, eyes that didn't cooperate with each other—her left eye often closed when her right one was wide open. Her occasional distorted facial expressions did not compliment her in the least. But I loved her anyway. I knew the sweetheart she had been. She was my second-born, and I loved her.

Passing the time in Sheila's room, I often sang "Jesus Loves Me" in her ear. I quoted scripture verses. I gave her facials. I rubbed her arms and legs, and cut her nails. I combed her hair, and plucked her stray eyebrows. We listened to Christian radio, tapes, and CDs.

THOSE WHO CARED FOR SHEILA

There was a constant turnover of caregivers in the facility, especially in the early years of Sheila's residency there. Pay was low and the work was hard, so aides didn't hang around long if they could find something better. We continually had to educate new personnel on how we wanted Sheila cared for, and what we expected from them. Yes, the facility trained them when they hired in and afterward on a continual basis, but we trained them too, in the specifics that were important to us. They were there to care for Sheila and we watched to see that they did.

Throughout Sheila's nearly twenty-six years of residency in the Skilled Nursing Facility, we maintained good harmony with the staff. Most of them were beautiful and caring people.

Because Sheila had been employed at the Reed City Hospital before her injury, she seemed to be a favorite. She was favored also, I think, because of her age, her condition, and her helplessness. Another factor possibly figuring into that attitude may have been her inability to express herself. She couldn't let a caregiver know if she was unhappy with the treatment she had received, like many other residents could, and sometimes did. One other thing included in that whole picture was our visibility. Clois and I were there often. The staff knew we loved her. There is no question about it—our presence and love for Sheila influenced the attitude of those who cared for her day after day.

Jesus, Please Rock Her For Me

When you were just a tiny one
I cradled you in my arms
And rocked you in my rocking chair,
Captured by your charms.

I held you close and sang to you.
You snuggled close to my breast,
Contented like a little chick
'Neath mama's wing in the nest.

How sweet to hold and rock you
Long ago in that old rocking chair.
Your tiny hand would reach up to my face—
I remember breathing a prayer—

"Dear Lord, Thank You for this little one.
It's a joy to hold her and bounce her on my knee.
Thank You, Lord, for sending her to bless us.
She's very special to Daddy and me.

"Please give us wisdom to train and teach her.
We need Your guidance. We don't want to fail.
Lead us, Lord, in the busyness of living,
Little by little may we see Your plan unveil."

The years passed by—my baby's now a lady.
Where did the time go? It seems much too soon—
Just yesterday I cuddled and rocked her
And sang her a lullaby tune.

Today if I could, I'd hold her and rock her,
I'd sing her another lullaby tune.
I'd soothe her hurts and fix everything
And she would feel better soon.

But she's too big for me to hold
And rock in my rocking chair.
"Dear Jesus, will You rock her for me?
Will You make her hurts easier to bear?

"And when she reaches for You,
Like she did when a baby, reaching for my face,
Gently take hold of her hand so she'll know
You are with her in life's dark, lonely place.

"We know she'll be safe, held close in Your arms,
In Your wisdom and sovereignty.
It's a comfort to know You are holding her—
There's no place more secure for anyone to be."

WILL THIS JOURNEY EVER END?

"Lord, it seems like it's time for You to take Sheila home. I don't understand why You leave her here, year after year. It took a long time for me to come to the place that I could ask You to take her. You know that, Lord. You have known the depth of my sorrow and heartache. And You know my thoughts now. It seems like Sheila has suffered long enough—too long. But You see the whole picture. I know that, and I trust You. I know it will be hard when Sheila leaves us, but I voice my heart, Holy Father. I think it's time for You to take Sheila home. You are Sovereign, and I leave her in Your love and care, and in Your timing. I praise Your name, Holy Father."

After years of being fed with an abdominal feeding tube, Sheila developed stomach problems that sometimes worsened, resulting in profuse vomiting. Her vomit was described as coffee grounds—dark brown, indicative of old blood. The surgeon suggested doing a scope to accurately diagnose the problem. We declined, feeling it would be useless to determine the problem and not do what needed to be done to address it. Years had passed since Sheila's injury, and we had made the decision not to employ any drastic means of treatment for her. Sheila's doctor treated her conservatively. Her stomach would heal, evidently, at least for a while, and she would appear to be comfortable again.

In the spring of 2001 Sheila began vomiting the brown, coffee ground material again. She developed pneumonia—very likely, aspiration pneumonia. We stayed by her side, thinking for sure we were going to lose her. She labored to breathe. Watching her was very difficult. After several days of struggling, Sheila once again pulled through.

Christmas morning 2002, we received a call from the Skilled Nursing Facility. "Sheila had a hard night," her nurse said. "She isn't doing well this morning."

"Please keep us informed," I told Jan. "We'll be here if she needs us. I'm getting Christmas dinner. We'll run up later, and see how she's doing." (We had moved into town in 1988, and were only six blocks away.)

I continued to prepare dinner for company, a total of ten. All was running smoothly. We were putting dinner on the table when the phone rang. Sheila had just been rushed to the emergency room. Clois, Pastor and his wife, and I jumped in the car and hurried to the emergency room. Dark brown, coffee ground vomit was flowing from Sheila again. It just kept coming.

Sheila's doctor was awaiting us. "Doctor, you know how we

feel. Our main goal is to keep Sheila comfortable. We don't want any drastic measures performed for her." Being very compassionate, he understood our feelings.

By this time Karen had arrived at the emergency room. Because she lived in Ohio she seldom had an opportunity to talk with the doctor. She had some questions for him, and expressed her desires regarding her sister's care. We were thankful she was home at that time.

Sheila's vomiting gradually lessened. The doctor made the decision to transfer her to the acute care department of the hospital, feeling the nursing staff there would be better equipped to keep close watch over her. After a couple nights there, Sheila was transferred back to the Skilled Nursing Facility. She miraculously, almost totally on her own, bounced back from that flare-up. For some reason, God brought her through again.

On the morning of April 20, 2004, we received a call from Sheila's nurse. Sheila was vomiting again. I told the nurse I would be there shortly. When I arrived, Sheila's doctor was at the nurses' desk. He told me what was going on with Sheila.

"Doctor, I'd like to talk to Clois to make sure he agrees, but I don't think we want any medical intervention for Sheila at this time, except for her comfort."

"Can you contact Clois?" he asked.

"Yes, I think I can reach him," I responded.

"Give him a call, and make sure you are together on this."

From the phone at the nurses' station, I called the Christian camp where Clois works two days a week. He finally came on the line. I filled him in. Clois had struggled with this decision, when we discussed it from time to time, but when I told him what was going on with Sheila, he agreed—just keep her comfortable.

On Friday, April 23, Clois left me at the Skilled Nursing

Facility to be with Sheila, and he drove the eighty miles to the prison to see Steve. We wanted Steve to know his sister was seriously ill. I sat with Sheila throughout the day. I told her I loved her. I told her she was beautiful. Strains of soft music flowed from her CD player, as words of the songs lifted praise to God. I hoped Sheila would feel a bit comforted by the music, and sense God's Presence in her room. I hoped she would feel my presence—whether she recognized me as Mom or not. I hoped she wasn't feeling alone.

Sheila was on the full amount of oxygen, with a monitor displaying her oxygen level and heart rate constantly. Robert, her day nurse, was in often to check on her. Aides came in every two hours to reposition her.

Clois returned at seven that evening. That was the scheduled time for the aides to come back to reposition Sheila. They came in at 7:10, and we stepped out while they made her comfortable. When they were done we went back into the room. Immediately two nurses, Natalie and Jessica, came in. They checked Sheila over briefly, and left.

Natalie returned a few minutes later. "The girls gave me a report after they repositioned Sheila. I wanted to check out for myself, what they told me. Then I called the doctor." She looked from Clois to me. "Doctor said this may be the night Sheila leaves us. He wants to make sure you know what's going on."

I slumped down, laid my head on the bed, and sobbed. Natalie came to my side, "I'm so sorry, Bev," she said.

It was approximately 7:40 now. Natalie informed us of some measures and medications the doctor had prescribed to keep Sheila as comfortable as possible. Then she left us alone.

Clois and I sat by Sheila's bed. I leaned over and laid my cheek on hers. "I love you, Sheila," I told her again. We sat quietly, observing her, watching her monitor closely. Natalie returned to administer the prescribed medication, and left.

HEALED AT LAST

During the last two hours we had witnessed slight seizure activity in Sheila, so we had no music playing in her room, to provide a quiet atmosphere. Clois and I sat there, voicing scattered comments of Sheila's long journey, and ours. As we talked and watched, we noticed on Sheila's finger monitor that her heart rate was slowing down. Clois walked out into the hall and told Natalie. Both she and Jessica came rushing in. Jessica sat down at Sheila's side and checked her pulse. We watched the monitor, as Sheila's heart rate continued to drop. In a matter of minutes the monitor went blank. Jessica nodded her head. At 8:40 p.m. Sheila was gone.

KAREN WAS ON HER WAY

Karen was on her way from Ohio, hoping to be with Sheila when she died, should this be the time. She had planned to leave home earlier, but had to take her son Scott to the doctor before she could head north. He had been out of school all week, and wasn't getting better.

After Sheila passed away we called Mark, our son-in-law. He had just talked to Karen and told us she was still an hour away. He said he would call her again, to tell her Sheila was gone, and that we would wait at the hospital for her.

After waiting inside for a while, Clois went out into the parking lot to watch for Karen. She arrived at 10:00 p.m. It was so good to see her. We walked to Sheila's room. The nurses' aides had prepared Sheila for our visit. They had selected her pretty blue dress to put on her. They had combed her hair, styled it into one big braid on her left side. Soft music was floating from her CD player. They were so anxious to help us, and please us.

This was it—the end of Sheila's long and tragic earthly journey. Tragic—that is how it appeared to us, anyway. How I would miss her, even in her comatose state. Yes, we would all miss her, but we knew what awaited Sheila at the end of her long journey. Heaven! Jesus awaited her! We rejoiced for her, our tears of sorrow mingling with our tears of celebration. She had finally reached her goal! Sheila was home! She was healed at last!

SHEILA'S MEMORIAL SERVICE

On April 27, 2004 we held Sheila's memorial service. We celebrated her life and her healing. The comments that came to us from those who remembered her in health, blessed us. There was a common thread that connected them all—her kind spirit, her concern for the needs of others, her ready smile, and her faith. And from the comments of her caregivers, we knew Sheila had somehow touched their hearts too, most of whom had not known her before she was injured.

A few days after Sheila's death we received a card from her cousin. Diane wrote, "Sheila had a very unique ministry." That captured my attention! Oh! Could it be? I mulled that statement over and over in my head. I thought of the many comments we had heard. Could it be? We had prayed time and time and time again that caregivers would sense something different about Sheila every time they went in to care for her. What would that difference be? God's Presence—His Spirit. We had prayed the hearts of her caregivers would be touched by the music in Sheila's room—the CDs and tapes we provided, and Christian radio. (We requested that her radio be tuned to one of two Christian stations at all times.) Could it be that Sheila had a ministry? Yes! It could be! "Thank You, Holy Father!"

OUR LETTER TO SHEILA

(The following letter was included in the bulletin for Sheila's memorial service.)

Dear Sheila,

Today we say our final earthly good-bye to you. It was hard Friday night when we were told, "It looks like Sheila may leave us tonight." We were torn between releasing you to be free from your bondage and our desire to hold onto you, but that decision was not ours to make. For almost nineteen years we loved you and enjoyed your vivacious spirit, your ready smile, your spunk, and your sweetness. Then one night came that devastating call from the emergency room in Big Rapids, "Your daughter has been severely injured in a car accident." The doctor asked permission to transfer you to Grand Rapids. He told us it was very icy and that we should stay home until the roads cleared. We knelt by the davenport and asked God to take care of you. We couldn't be with you right then, but we knew He could.

The journey since that time has been long. There have been many questions and no answers. We had to give up the Sheila we had known, and love and accept the Sheila you had become—totally incapacitated.

How many times Mom stood at your bedside, stroked your forehead, rubbed your arms, combed your hair, gave you facials and quoted the 23rd Psalm, and sang "Jesus Loves Me" in your ear. Sometimes your facial expression seemed to reveal a relaxing response. Naturally, it was easier for Mom to do the "girl" things for you, than it was for Dad, but you were still his "little girl."

We had hoped that one day Dad would walk you down the aisle—his "little girl" now a beautiful bride, dressed in her lovely wedding gown—and give you away to some deserving young knight, but that was not to be, for some reason we will never know. Rather, here we are today, at your funeral service saying good-bye. There will be a vacancy in our lives, but we'll be okay. It hurts having you go, but we also have feelings of celebration and anticipation for you, because today we know you are with Jesus! According to what we read in the Bible, you now have a new body, Sheila! Hurrah for you, sweetie! So what we are really doing today is celebrating your healing! Yes, we're celebrating! Sheila is finally healed!

Thank you for being the sweetheart you were. You have touched many lives. God has used you and your journey in more ways than we could ever imagine. Watch for us, Sheila. We'll join you one of these days. We love you,

Mom & Dad

Dear Lord,
You cover me with warmth,
peace, and contentedness,
like Grandma's handmade quilt.
Thank You!

LIFE GOES ON

What a long journey we traveled with Sheila. It was a moment-by-moment, day-by-day journey that unbelievably stacked up to twenty-six years and twenty days. There are many unknowns, many questions, and no answers. I don't spend much time there, looking for answers. I will never know the why of Sheila's injury and resulting long journey. But, as I have searched and studied in "God's Training School" on my journey over the last twenty-six years, I've come to understand the better thing is just to trust God. That's where I find peace. Peace has a high price tag. People would give an arm and a leg, if such sacrifice would bring peace.

STEVE'S JOURNEY ISN'T OVER

We're still on the long journey with Steve. In many ways, his journey will never end. But he has a wonderful traveling companion. God's Holy Presence is with him always, everywhere. He is never away from God's lingering Presence! What a strength and comfort that is! What peace that provides—for him and for Clois and me. His hope is in God. Steve is living for Jesus right where he is. *"Thank You, Lord!"*

Life is different for us, because of Sheila's long journey, and Steve's incarceration. Their life situations have surely limited our number of grandchildren. Perhaps we would experience fewer lonely times had their situations been different. But again—it does no good for us to focus on what might have been. So I give that package to God, too, and trust Him.

God is good. We have seen many blessings along the way. Our family is following God—Steve, Karen; her husband, Mark; and their boys, Andy and Scott. What greater blessing could there be? I can never praise God enough for His Presence, His blessings, and His wonderful ministry to me.

A LETTER OF APPRECIATION

A couple of months after Sheila's death, I told Karen I wanted to write a letter of appreciation to her dad's and my siblings and their families, thanking them for supporting us throughout Sheila's hospitalization. Karen said she had been thinking about writing a letter too. I organized my thoughts and put them on paper. Karen and Steve each wrote a note to add to mine. I would like to share these with you.

August 16, 2004

Dear Family,

It was a short time ago that Clois and I sat by Sheila's bed as she said good-bye to this world and made the transition to her eternal home. It was heartbreaking to see her go, but we know where she is. She is in the presence of Jesus, where she will be forever. We are thankful she is done with her pain and suffering, but we certainly miss her. How thankful we are that through the years we did our best to help her lay a foundation that prepared her to die, as well as to live.

At Sheila's memorial service a few comments were made about the person she was. More comments have come to us. We want to honor her, by sharing some of them with you.

A businessman from our town, who remembers Sheila as a school classmate, told our neighbor this: "I think Sheila was the sweetest, friendliest girl I ever met. I don't think she had an enemy in the world."

Another man who remembers her from school: "I used to sit and look at Sheila, and wonder what was different about her. I knew she was a friend of my cousins. They were Christians, so I thought maybe she was, too. My family soon moved away. After a while, I became a Christian. I think Sheila was my first introduction to Jesus."

A young woman from our church: "I started coming to youth meetings here, when Sheila was part of that group. She was always the one that included me. She would call me over to join in the fun. She wanted to make sure I wasn't left out. I wanted to stand up at her memorial service and tell everyone, but I didn't."

Clois had a mid-June appointment with our doctor, and Sheila's. He said to Clois, "Sheila was a Christian, wasn't she?" Clois told him she was, and proceeded to tell him some of the statements about her, that had come to us. He thanked Clois for sharing those comments. He said they gave him a better understanding of who Sheila was. We wondered what had drawn him to the conclusion that Sheila was a Christian. We hadn't told him, and he had never known Sheila before her injury. Maybe things he saw in her room . . . perhaps the music he heard there . . . or the prayers we prayed that God's Spirit would be present there, that Sheila's caregivers would notice something different . . .

Diane, Sheila's cousin, wrote that Sheila had a very unique ministry. Three weeks after Sheila's death I, Bev, held a session at a ladies' retreat at Spring Hill camp. Referring to Diane's statement, Denise, wife of the president of Spring Hill, told me of a booklet written a few years ago titled "The Power of the Powerless." She said the booklet delivered such a powerful message that one of the leading newspapers published it in its entirety. Sheila was powerless for twenty-six years, but somehow God used her to proclaim His message. Yes, from what we have seen and heard, that is true.

We were privileged to have Sheila in good health for almost nineteen years. What a heartbreak her accident was, and her resultant severe injury. It was a crisis heartbreak that extended into twenty-six long years of day-by-day heartache. Looking back, it seems unbelievable that she was comatose for that long. But it stacked up a day at a time, mounting up to twenty-six years! During those years Sheila appeared to be fairly comfortable most of the time, for which we are very thankful. But we know she had to be suffering to some degree, just lying in bed for such a long time.

We are thankful we loved our injured Sheila, just as we loved our healthy Sheila. We have no regrets. Neither do we have answers. We only know God is sovereign, and He is a God of love. He has been faithful through it all, and He will be faithful in the tomorrows.

We are blessed by God to have Karen for a daughter. When Mark came into the picture, he became one of our own, and we are thankful for him. Karen is a beautiful person, and a good mother to their sons—Andy and Scott. We are very thankful for our grandsons. They are precious young men. Mark is a faithful and supportive husband and a great father, for which we are thankful.

We are thankful for Steve. He has been a blessing to us time and time again. Yes, he took us places we didn't want to go. But there is no question that God is working in Steve's life. We recently heard this statement: "Parents think of parenting as a sprint. It isn't a sprint. It's a marathon." Yes, Steve had trouble with the sprint, but he's going to be a winner in the marathon, with God's help.

We want to express appreciation to all of our siblings and their spouses, nieces, nephews . . . on and on it goes. You are very special to us. It's wonderful to know you celebrate with us, and hurt with us. We were happy to see so many of Sheila's cousins at the funeral home, and at her memorial service. Thank you. Your presence and support were a blessing. Sheila has been out of circulation for a long time, and it was great to see that you had not forgotten her.

Sincerely,
Bev and Clois

A NOTE FROM KAREN

It has been just over three months now since Sheila went home to heaven. It was more difficult than I had imagined. I expected relief to come with the realization that she was no longer suffering. But the memories of who she was, things we did as a family, and how things might have been were, at times, overwhelming. Most of my grieving took place in the early years after Sheila's accident. Although you don't ever "get over" such a tragedy, you do eventually heal. Death is always sobering. It reminds me that we are all fragile mortal beings, and demands that I evaluate my own life and priorities. Even when it's expected and welcomed, death is heavy and emotionally/physically draining.

Whether you knew it or not, God used you to minister to us. Your company and support helped us. We enjoyed hearing your memories of Sheila. Some of you came in spite of physical limitations, some at considerable expense, and many took off work. You are all so very special. I may not be around to enjoy your company very much because of the distance between us, but I know that my extended family is a precious gift. More importantly, thank you for always being there for my parents. They, too, are precious people. They have maintained their relationship with each other and with our Lord Jesus under extreme situations. They have been faithful, loving parents through the tough stuff of life.

Because of our faith in Jesus Christ and all that He has done in our behalf, we have the hope of seeing Sheila again . . . whole and healed. I am looking forward to that day!

A NOTE FROM STEVE

II Corinthians 1:3-4 declares, "Blessed be God, even the Father of our Lord Jesus Christ, the Father of mercies, and the God of all comfort; Who comforteth us in all our tribulation, that we may be able to comfort them which are in any trouble, by the comfort wherewith we ourselves are comforted of God." In thinking about Sheila's life I have become very aware of how Father God has used Mom and Dad, Karen and Mark, other members of our family, and myself to minister comfort to others who have a loved one in a similar situation. Then after Sheila's promotion to glory, Father God has offered us yet another opportunity to comfort, encourage, and lift up others with our great hope—that hope that is based on our impending resurrection. Because Christ Jesus said " . . . I am the resurrection, and the life: he that believeth in me, though he were dead, yet shall he live: And whosoever liveth and believeth in me shall never die . . . " (John 11:25-26 KJV.)

THANK YOU ALL, AND GOD BLESS YOU!

*Because of Jesus,
every tomorrow is bright,
and full of promise!*

Prayer of Praise

During a period of several months, I wrote alphabetical lists in my journal titled, *WHAT GOD MEANS TO ME*. I was very selective with my words and phrases. I didn't include them just because they started with the proper letter. They expressed what I felt in my heart toward God. The following is my *PRAYER OF PRAISE*, using selections from my thirteen alphabetical lists.

Dear Father God,
    I praise You now because You are the AMAZEMENT in my life! You amaze me because You love me! You amaze me because way back there You made provision for the Holy Spirit to be present with me, and with all who serve You! You are my ANTICIPATION, Dear Lord! ANTICIPATION to know You better, and to one day see You face to face!

    Because of You, Holy Father, I have BUBBLES in my life! Effervescent BUBBLES of JOY OVERFLOWING! Even in the tough times, Dear Father God, You are there! The joy of that confidence is deep-seated and stabilizing. That confidence BLOWS BUBBLES OF JOY into my life! Thank You, Father!

CONSTANT, CONSISTENT CHALLENGE is always before me, Father God, to be more like Jesus! To know more about Jesus! I can never reach the peak! Thank You, Dear Father!

You DRESS ME IN YOUR RIGHTEOUSNESS! How can I thank You, Dear Father God, except to bow humbly before You and say yes to Your plan for my life! Because of You, Dear Father, I dare to rise each morning and say, "It's a good morning!" I dare to live, to smile, to sing! Thank You, Father God!

You are the END of my search, Dear Father. You are the EXTENDER OF MERCY! How can I praise You enough? You are my ENABLER! Thank You, Dear Father!

You are my FIRM FOUNDATION. When life is shaky, You are there, like a FLOWING WELL—ever giving, ever meeting me at the point of my need! You FILL ME WITH AWE, Dear Father God, my FATHER NOW AND FOREVER!

You provide for me a GARMENT OF PRAISE to wear, in the midst of hard situations. You are like GENTLE THUNDER BOOMS in my life—speaking, guiding softly and gently, but with powerful impact!

You are my HIDING PLACE, Dear Father God. My HEALER—from life's hurts and disappointments. You HOLD me, Father, when I would fall apart. You are the HALLELUJAH of my life!

You are the INVOLVED PRESENCE that makes a difference in my life! You INDWELL my heart! I long to worship You, Dear Father God!

JESUS! You are my personal friend! You bring JEWELS into my life—precious Jewels of Your Presence! Your love! Your assurance! You are JUST AWESOME, Dear Father God!

KING of my life, of my universe! You are the KEEPER of my heart! Of my peace! Father God, You KINDLE A FIRE within me for more of You!

You are the LORD of my life! You are LOVING arms around me, providing me with assurance that I can go on. You are my LIGHT IN THE DARKNESS! Praise Your name, Dear Father.

You are my MOLDER AND SHAPER, gently helping me to become more like Your pattern for me. You are a MAGNET, drawing me to Yourself. Thank You, Father.

You are the NURTURING PRESENCE in my life, growing me into what You want me to be. You are my NUDGE-GIVER, reminding me to be sensitive, to watch my tongue, to be patient. NAME ABOVE ALL NAMES, You have NO BEGINNING, NO END! Praise You, Father!

You are the ONE I RUN TO, Dear Lord. You are the ONE AND ONLY worthy of my life's devotion. You are the ORIGIN of everything good in my life.

Father God, You are the PROVIDER OF MY PEACE! My PURPOSE FOR LIVING! You PURCHASED my salvation with Your blood! You are the POWER OF THE RESURRECTION in my life! Thank You, Dear Father!

You QUIET MY HEART. You are a QUILT of warmth and at-homeness. You are the end of my QUEST, Father God.

My RENEWAL! My RESOURCE! My REASON FOR HOPE! My REASON TO REJOICE!

The SEEKER OF MY HEART! My SANCTUARY IN THE STORM! You lead me beside STILL WATERS! Thank You, Dear Father!

You are my TRAVEL AGENT on life's journey. The TENDERIZER of my heart and attitude, my gentle TEACHER.

You are my UNDERSTANDING, UNCHANGING, ULTIMATE FRIEND! My UNLIMITED RESOURCE!

VICTORIOUS FRIEND! The VOICE I HEAR IN the VALLEY times of my life. Thank You, Father God.

You WASH me and make me WHITER than snow, Your Word says, Dear Father. You are the WILLING provider of salvation. Father—You WERE, You are, and You WILL BE—forever!

You are my X-AMPLE, the X-CLAMATION point in my life, my X-PECTATION of a glorious future, the X-CITEMENT in my life! Thank You, Father God.

Father, YOU love me! Can it be? YOU died for me! Thank You! Thank You! You are my YEARNING HEART'S completion! YOU anticipate my praise! Awesome! YESTERDAY, today, and forever, Jesus is the same! Thank You, Father!

You are my ZEST for life! Thank You, Father, for sometimes ZIPPING MY LIPS! Thank You for ZEBRA-RECOGNITION, for helping me see the difference between black and white—between right and wrong.

Father God, You mean all of this to me, and more. I offer praise to You, simply, humbly, acknowledging that I need You. I cannot make it by myself, Dear Father. Thank You for being there! I offer myself to You, Dear Father—an offering to You. Praise Your Holy Name! Amen.

A Magnificent, Promise-Filled Rainbow

A brisk blowing breeze greeted the morning,
Dawning light revealed a dark, foreboding sky,
Anxiety was my heartfelt emotion—
Obvious in my worrisome sigh.

On schedule for the day was a boat ride,
An island visit to the west.
I hoped to travel on mirror-smooth water—
That's my choice when I'm a boat guest.

The boat first was loaded with lumber and cars,
Then for the islanders things brand new!
Finally passengers were invited to board,
So they climbed on board and we did, too.

The captain piloted the boat through the channel,
The ride was smooth, it was really great—
Until I remembered the wind and the sky—
I knew we wouldn't continue the smooth-sailing rate.

We reached the end of the quiet channel
Into belching waters of the stormy lake.
With each lurch of the western-bound vessel
I just knew my life was at stake.

The boat rose, confronting each wave,
Then sped forward and nose-down it fell.
One after another it met the challenge
Of each furious, white-capped swell.

Each wave made a great and powerful splash
The full length of the boat and as high.
It was frightening on the angry water
Beneath the dark, foreshadowing sky.

Memory found an appropriate song—
"Jesus, Please my Pilot be."
"O, Great Pilot," I breathed, "It's so stormy!
The water is rough and it frightens me!"

We sailed for an hour on the churning sea,
Then off in the west a good distance away
Peaked a thin line of pale-blue horizon—
It suggested a brighter, more enjoyable day.

We rocked and rolled with each lurch of the boat,
Not enjoying what was planned to be fun.
The pale-blue horizon slowly rose higher, then—
Wonderful surprise! Bright and beautiful sun!

The waves still swelled, the boat rose and fell,
The water still splashed by my window,
But now with each splash came a radiant blessing—
A magnificent, vanishing rainbow.

With promise of clear weather, calming wind,
Smooth sailing soon to be!
Promise of sunshine and quiet water—
An accommodating, friendly sea!

The unsettling part of the ride was over—
Enjoyment was on for the rest of the day.
The promise of the rainbow would be fulfilled,
For this time many folks had set aside to play.

* * * *

The harsh winds of reality charge into my life,
Swelling and churning like the raging sea—
Nearly capsizing my fragile lifeboat—
Not mirror-smooth like I wish life to be.

With each swelling, threatening life-splash
I turn to Jesus, the only true Resource I know.
Peace returns, as I hear Him gently whisper,
"Trust me, child. My plans include a rainbow."

Dear Reader . . .

Thank you for taking the time to read my heart. I have no doubt that you see it on every page of this book. My words make me vulnerable, I know, but I have felt compelled to share God's wonderful ministry.

As you read, you were walking alongside me, on my journey of life. This is my story, written from my own personal experience. Here and there throughout my writing I included Clois, Karen and her family, and Steve, but basically this is my story. We experienced it together, but we each dealt with it in our own way. The others could each write their stories, and they would be much different than mine. Yes, this one is mine. I lived it . . . hurt through it . . . struggled through it, and sometimes wondered if I would survive it. But God was faithful. He reminded me of Old Testament accounts. I remembered what kind of reputation He had. I began to rely on Him. He taught me, and I learned. I became better acquainted with Him.

My prayer is that every reader of this book will come to believe, beyond the shadow of a doubt, that God is faithful and trustworthy; that God is involved in the intimate details in the lives of each of His children. I pray you will face the difficulties of life differently after reading this book.

Early on my journey, eight to ten months into Sheila's injury, I made a discovery. Oh, I made many discoveries. You just read about them—but not this one. I discovered there are very few real questions in life—*real* questions. When a loved one is lowered, through sickness or accident, to the level of wondering about the future—life or death—when that is an unknown, there are few things that really matter, few questions. Those questions deal with eternal issues—God, assurance, the future, separation. And I made another discovery that goes right along with this one. The answers to those very few real questions of life are found in God's Word—the only source of stability for life!

I am not disappointed in my relationship with God these days, as I was in my earlier years. I have found Him to be sufficient. May you also find Him to be sufficient for all the concerns of your life.

Blessings!

About the Author

There are no letters following Bev Bowman's name to indicate college degrees she has earned. But, the school of life has its own way of teaching as one endures hard-life experiences. People can graduate from those experiences with honors, or they can fail miserably. It is one's response that makes the difference. Bev Bowman has earned some major life degrees—with honors.

In July 2005 Bev and her husband, Clois, will celebrate forty-nine years of marriage. They have three children and two grandchildren.

After raising their children, Bev did medical transcription for many years. She has also been a speaker for ladies' retreats, mother-daughter banquets, and other similar events.

To order copies of *Still Praising Him*, please contact:

Curtman Publishing

P.O. Box 275

Reed City, MI 49677

E-mail: cbhandyman@juno.com